This book belongs to :

_____

_____

_____

_____

_____

_____

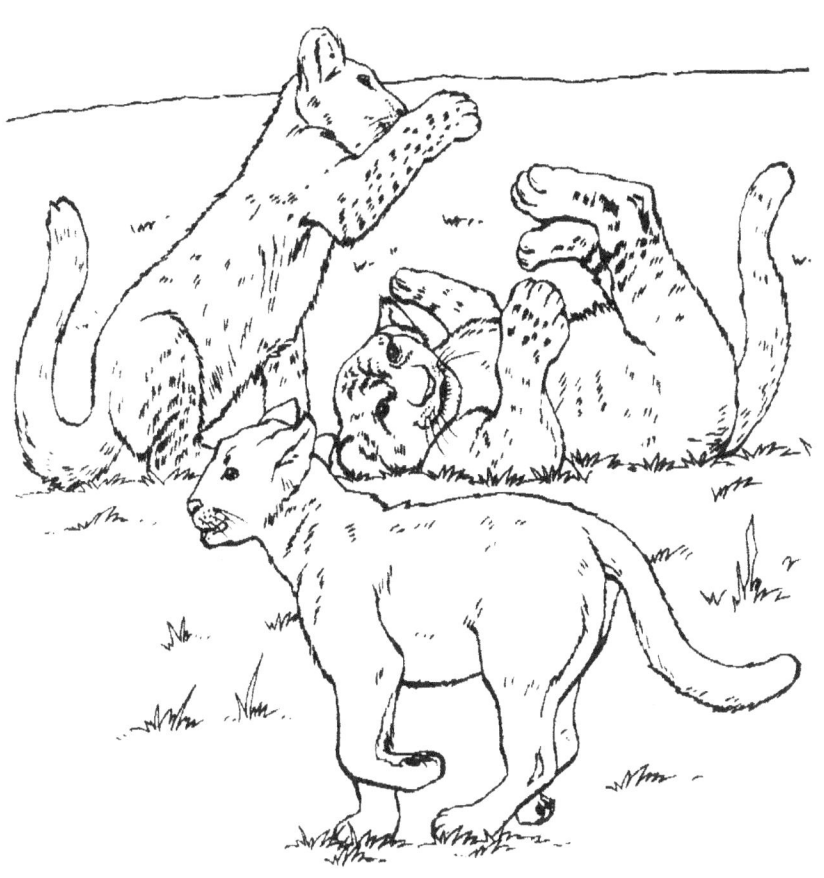

Lions

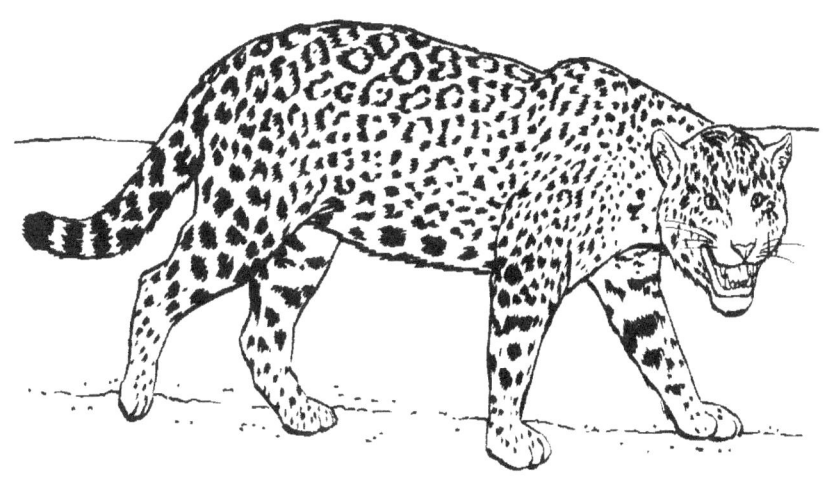

Jaguar

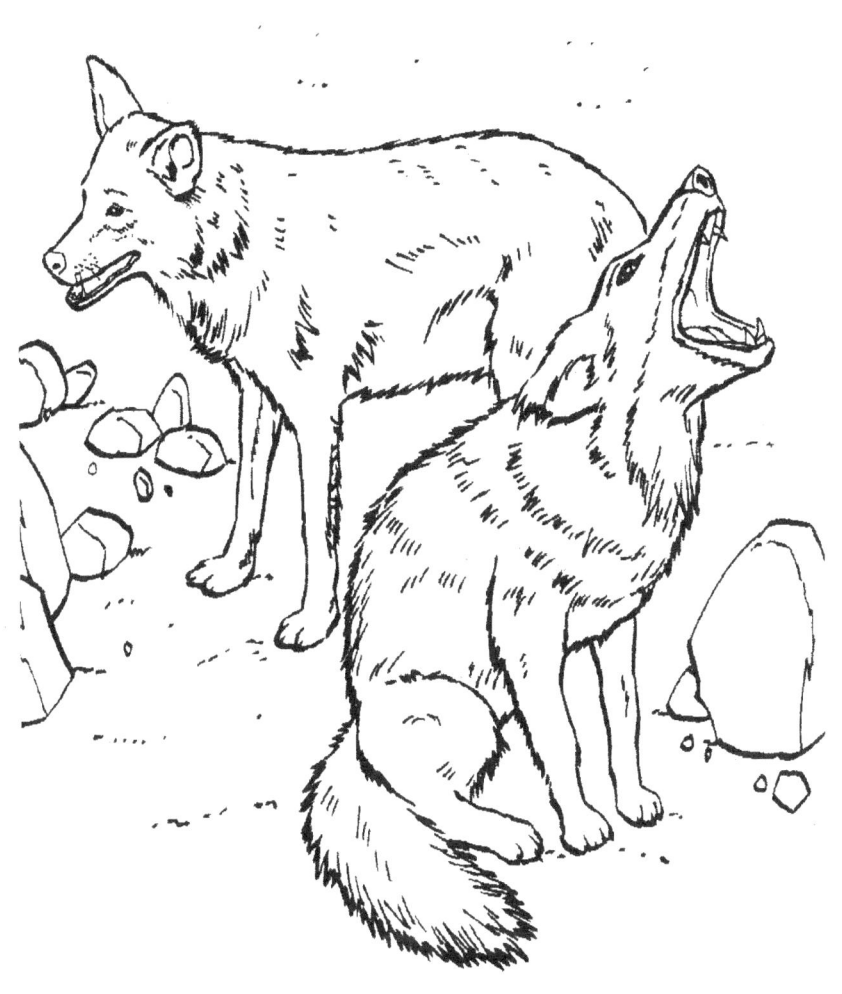

Coyotes are spread across Alaska, Canada, USA, Mexico, and Central America.

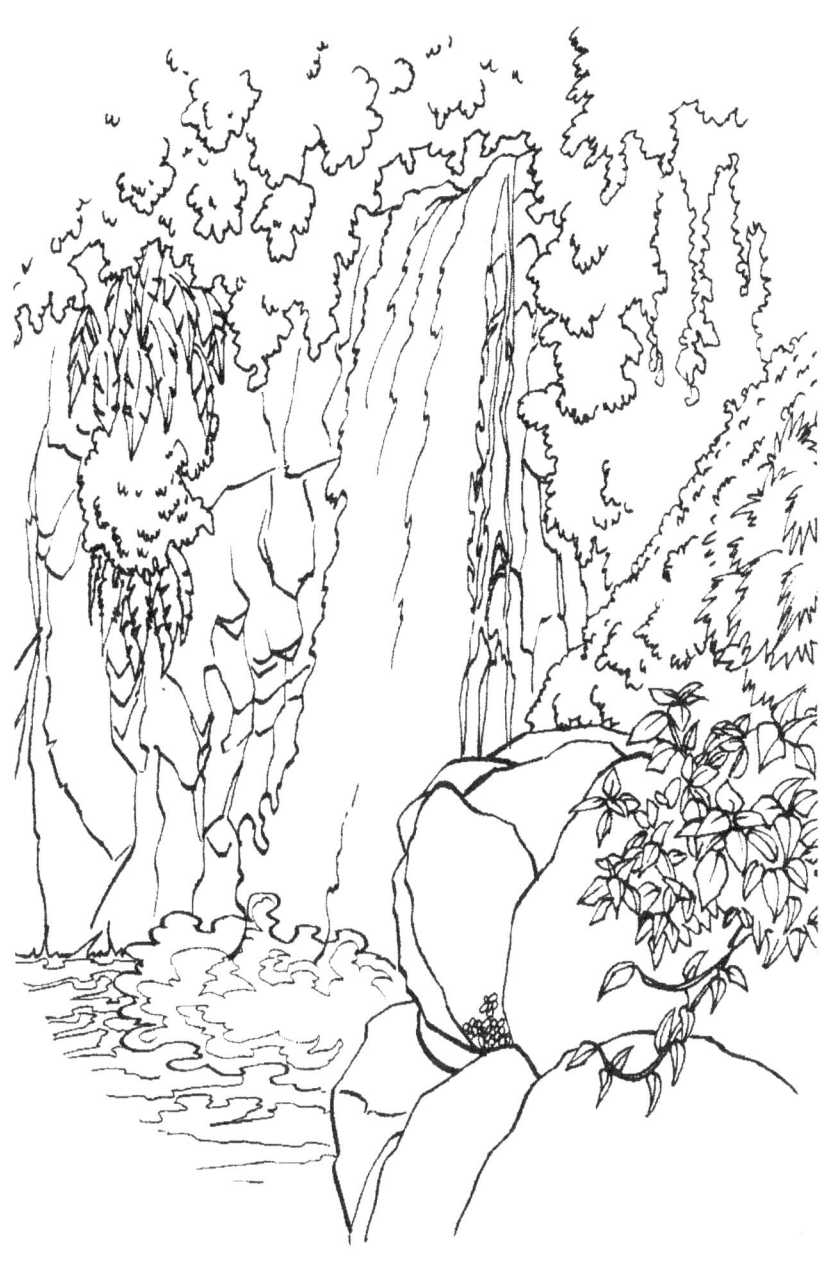

Waterfalls

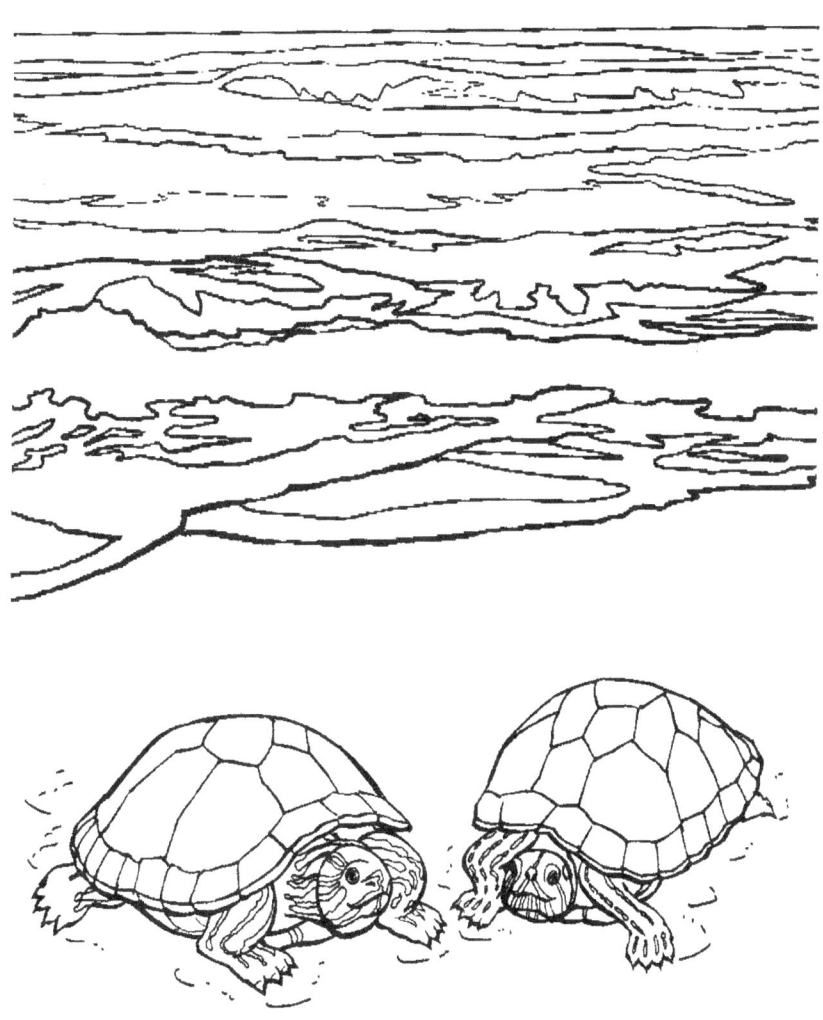

Turtles

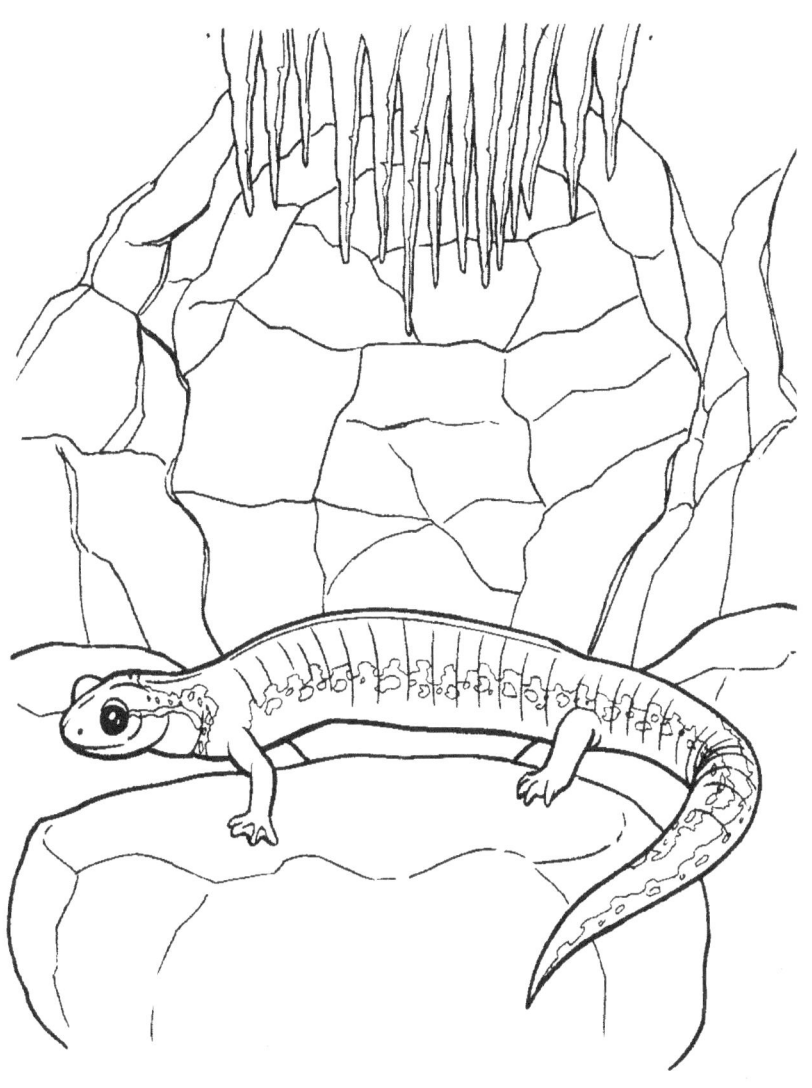

The cave salamander is able to survive for up to 6 years without food.

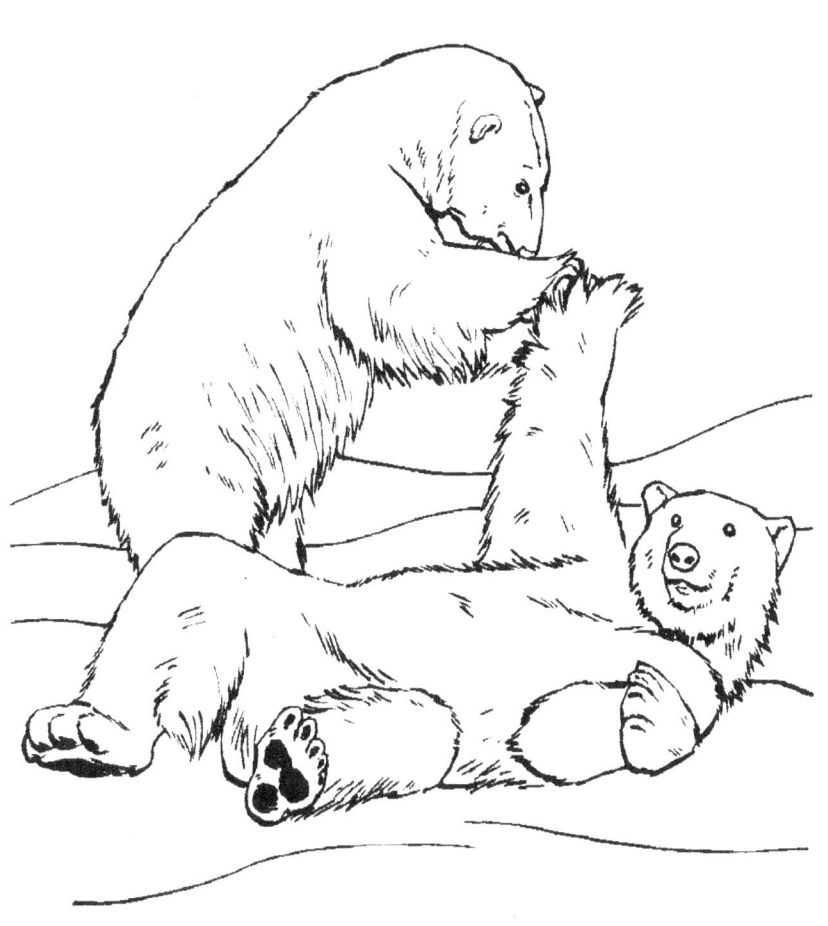

Polar Bears

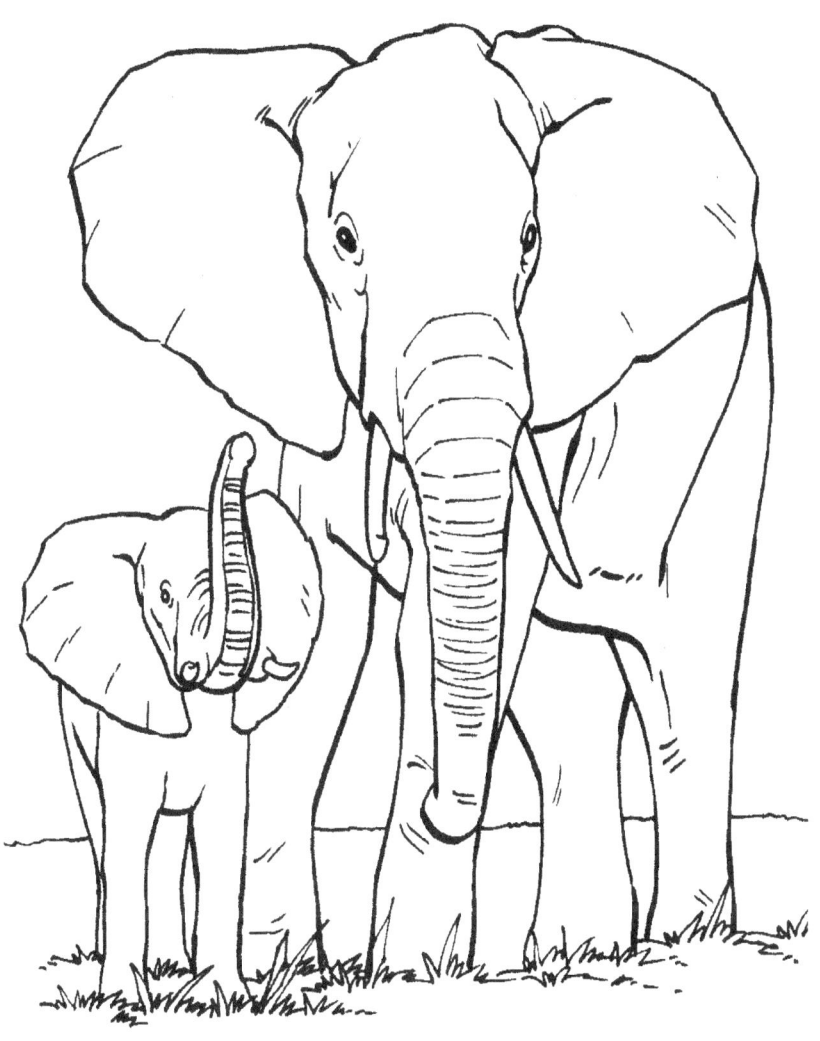

Elephants' ears are so big to help keep them cool.

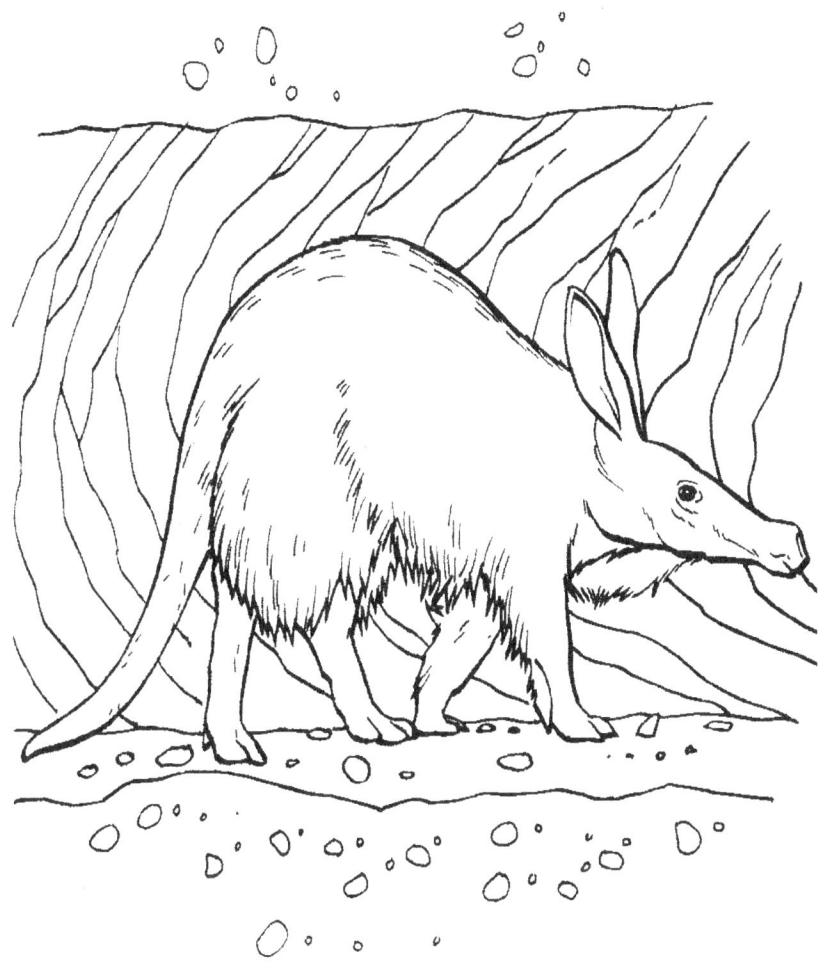

Aardvark

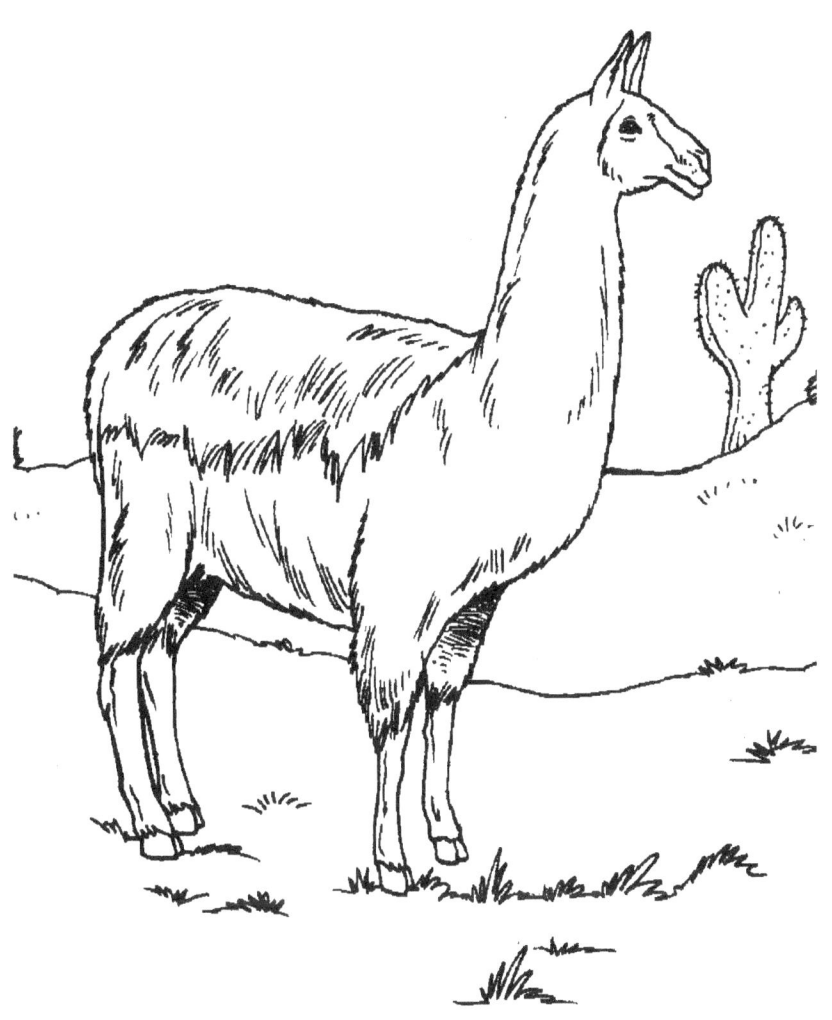

Llama

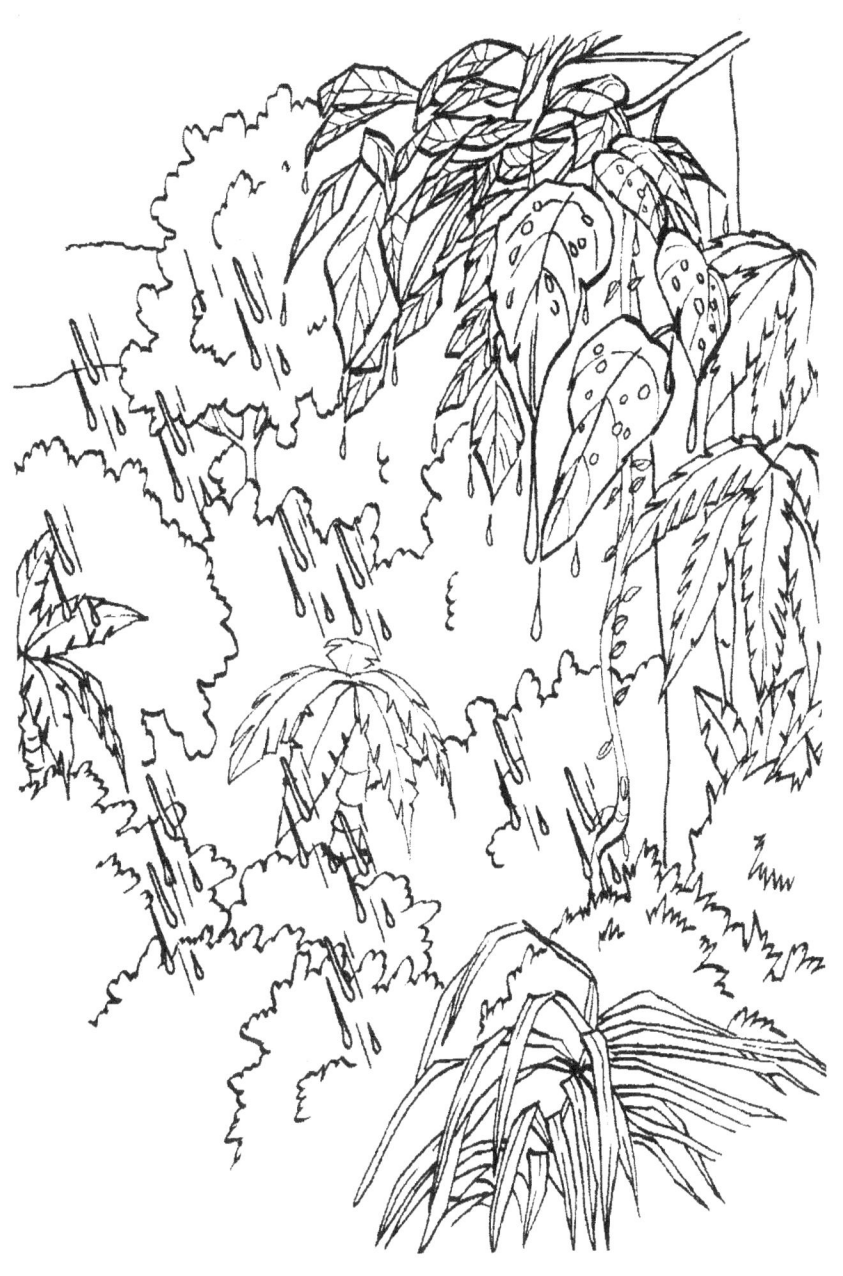

It rains every day in the rainforest.

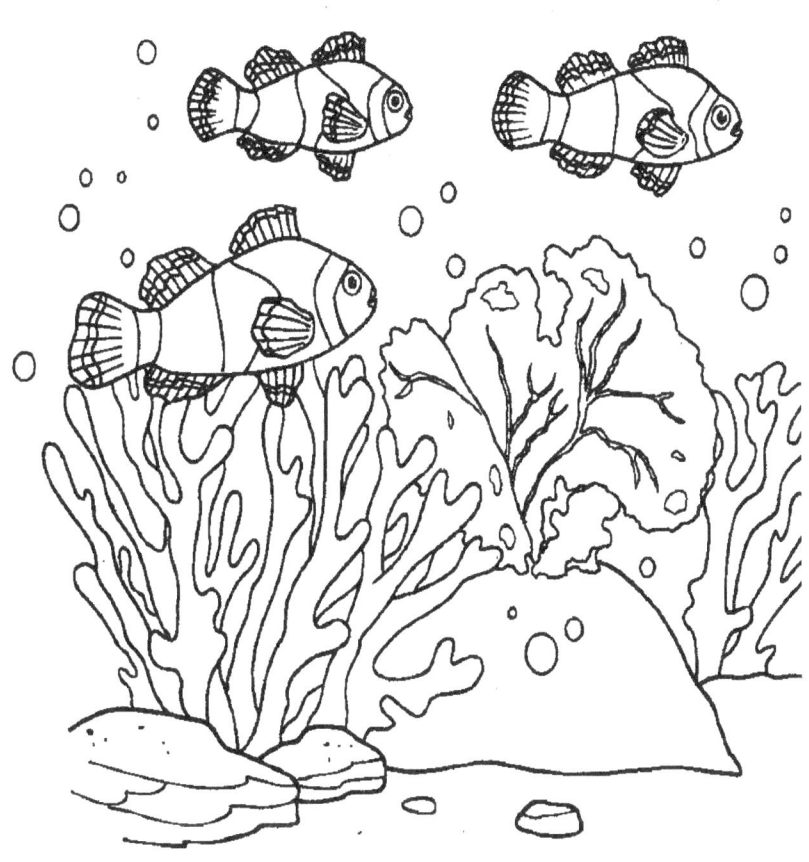

Clownfish

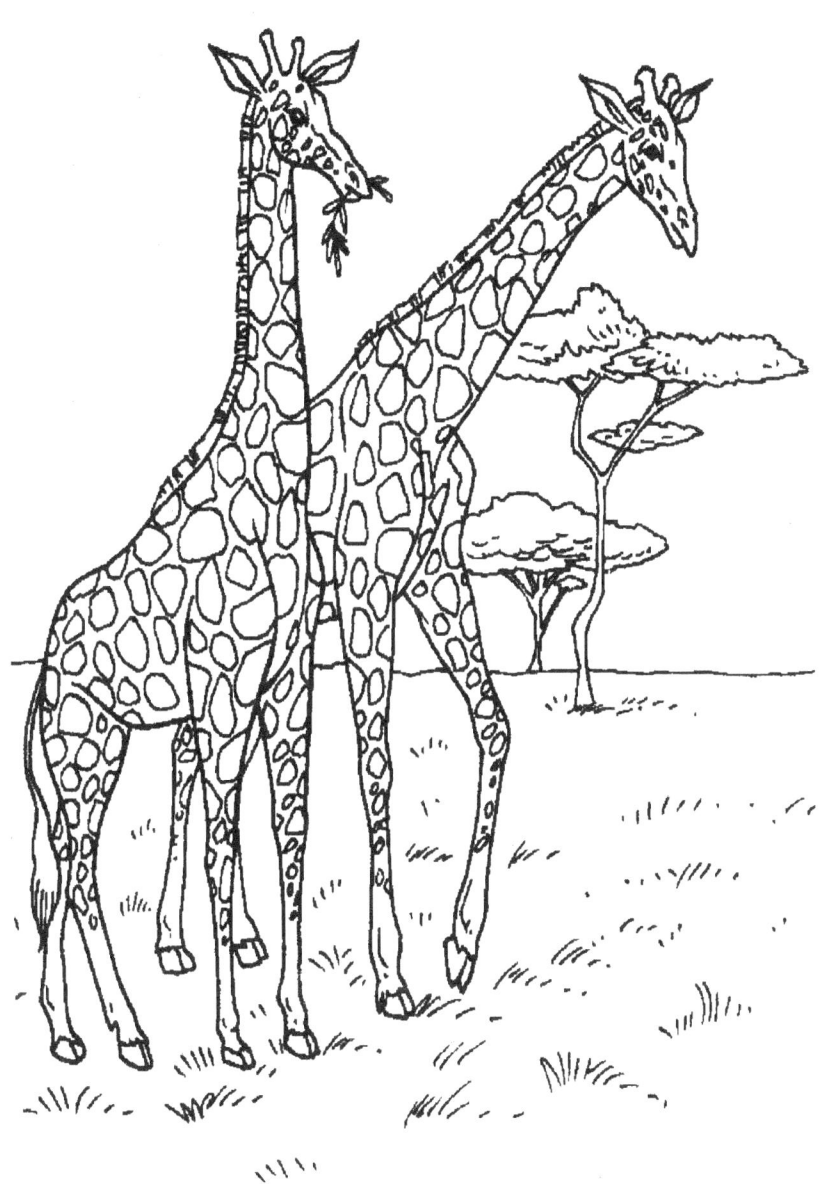

Giraffes

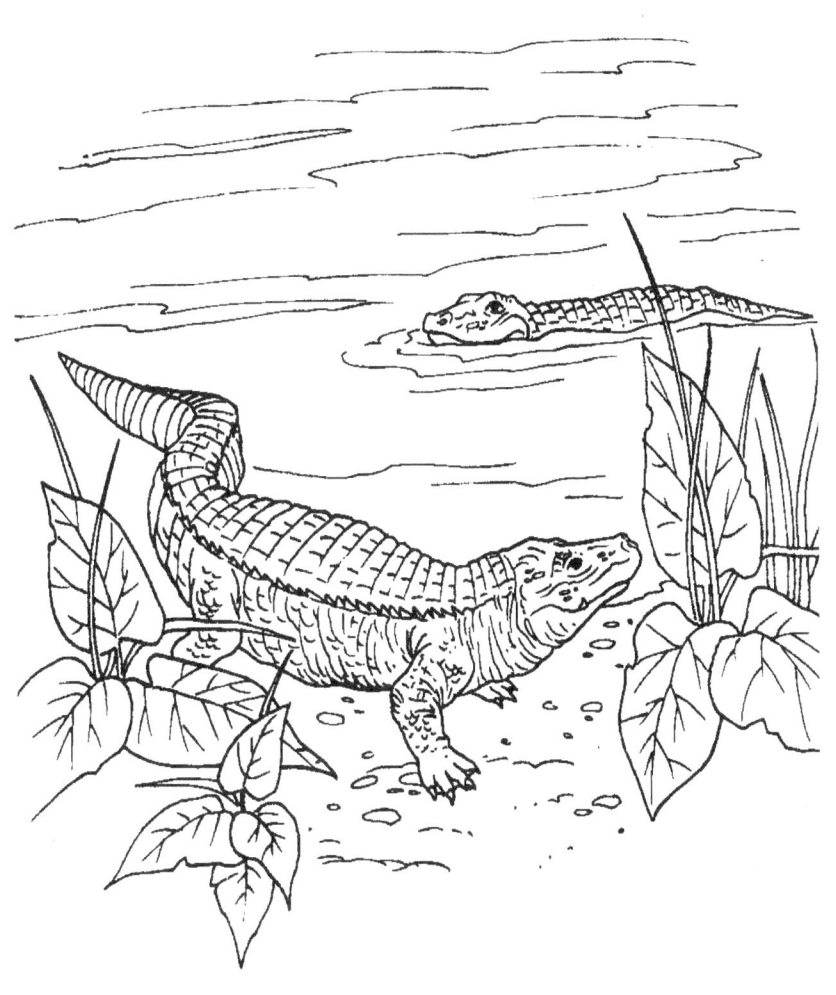

Alligators

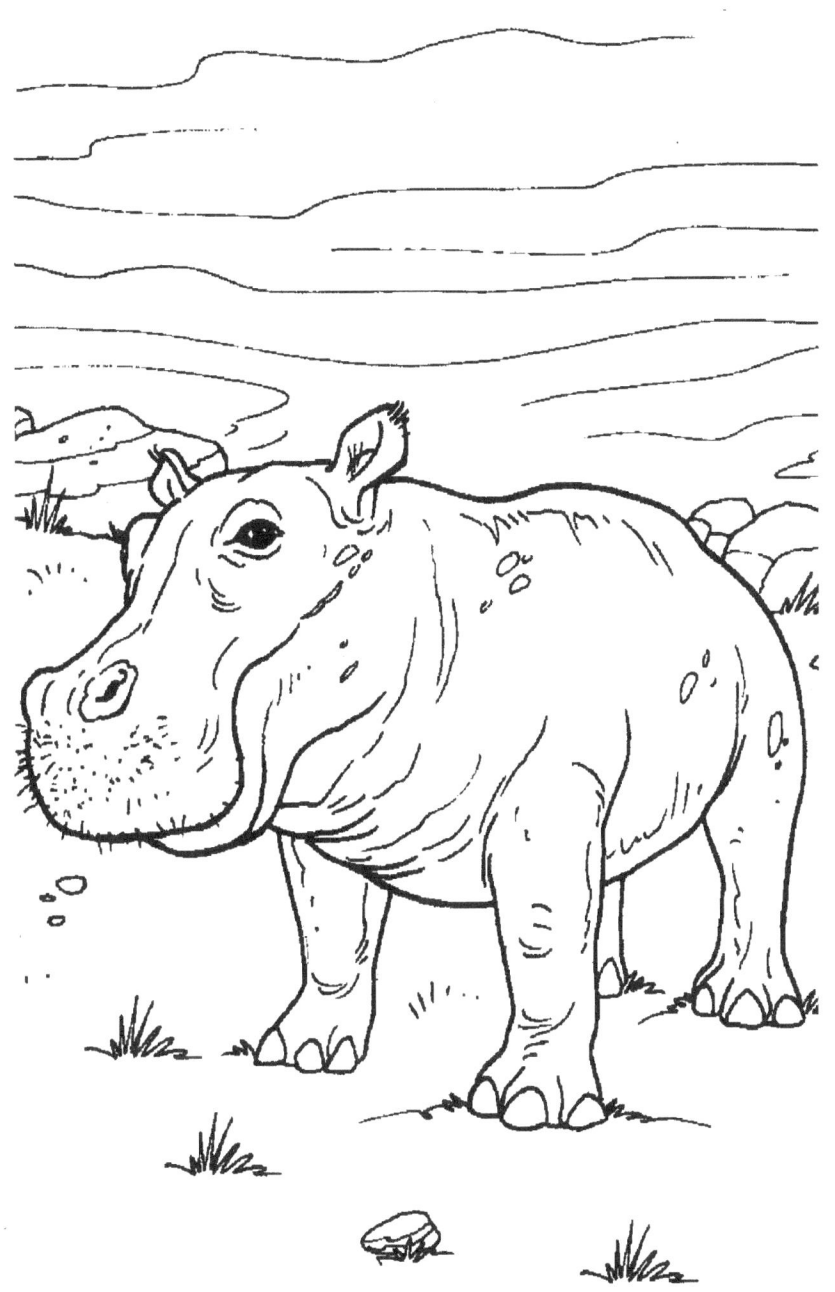

Hippopotamus

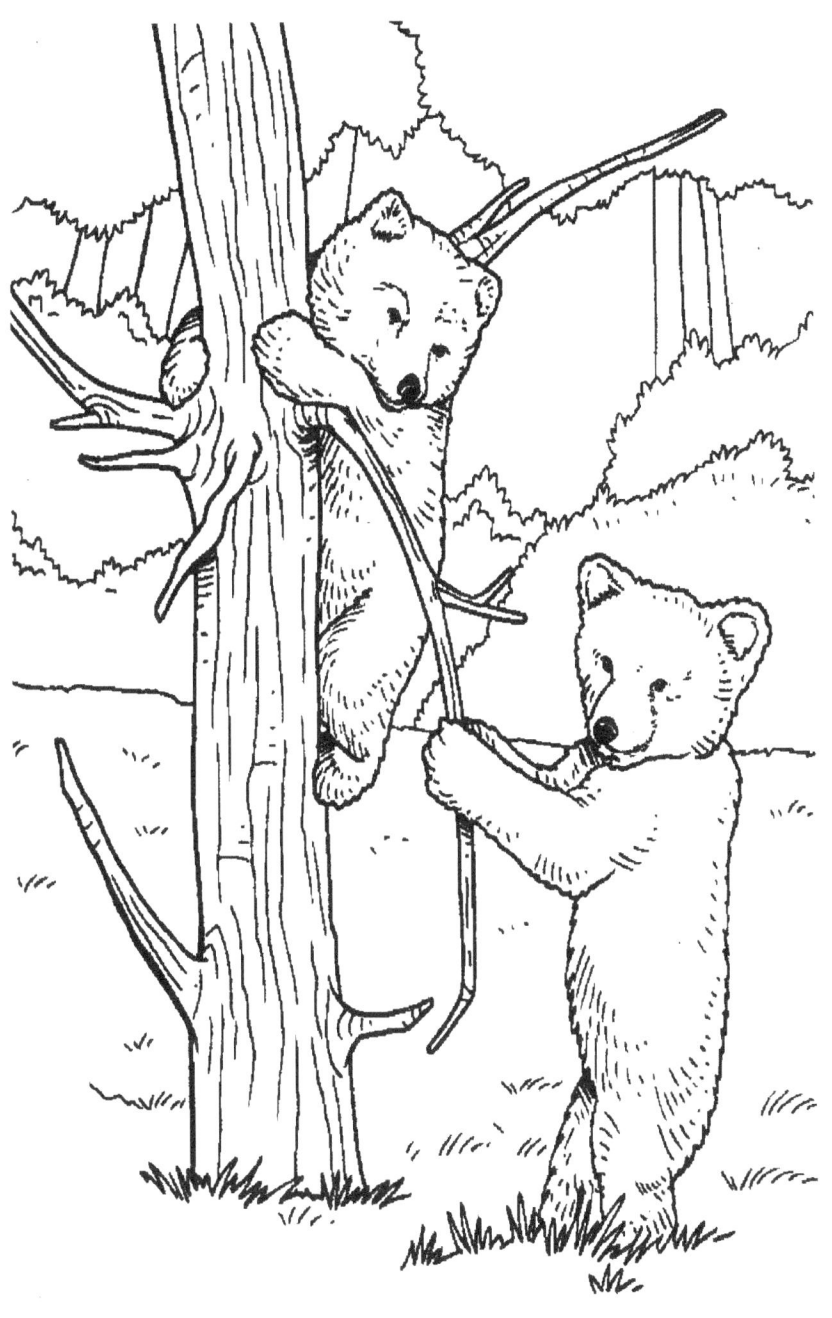

Bear Cubs

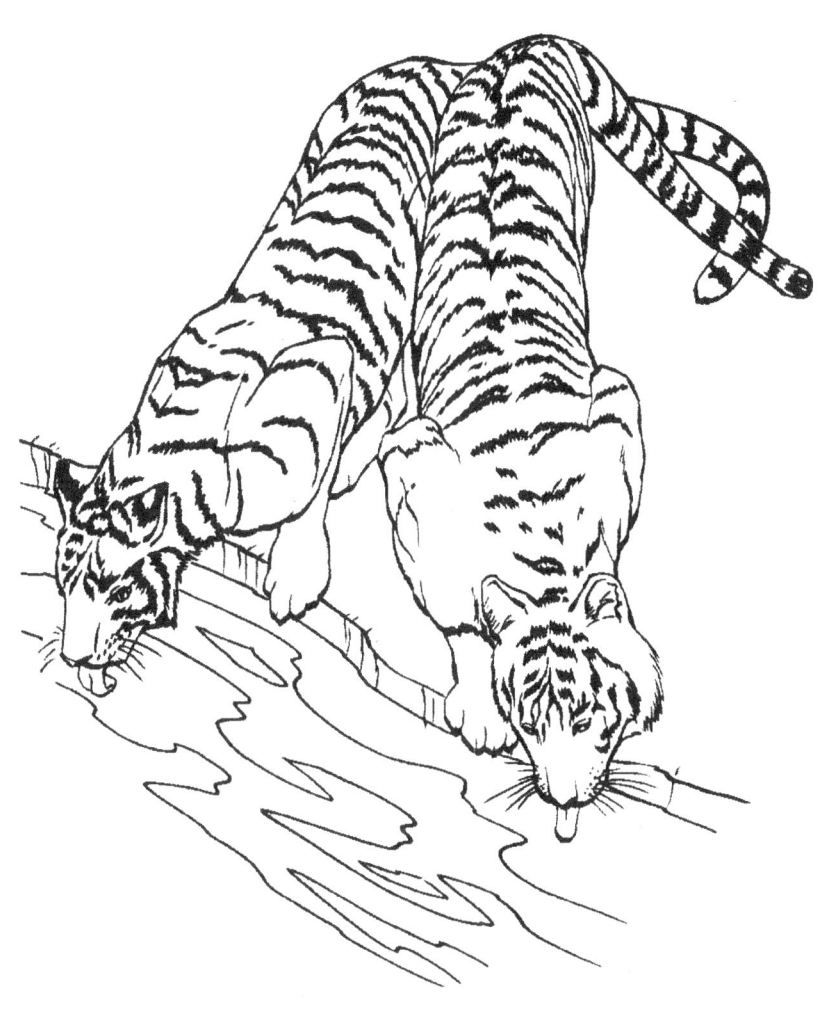

Tigers

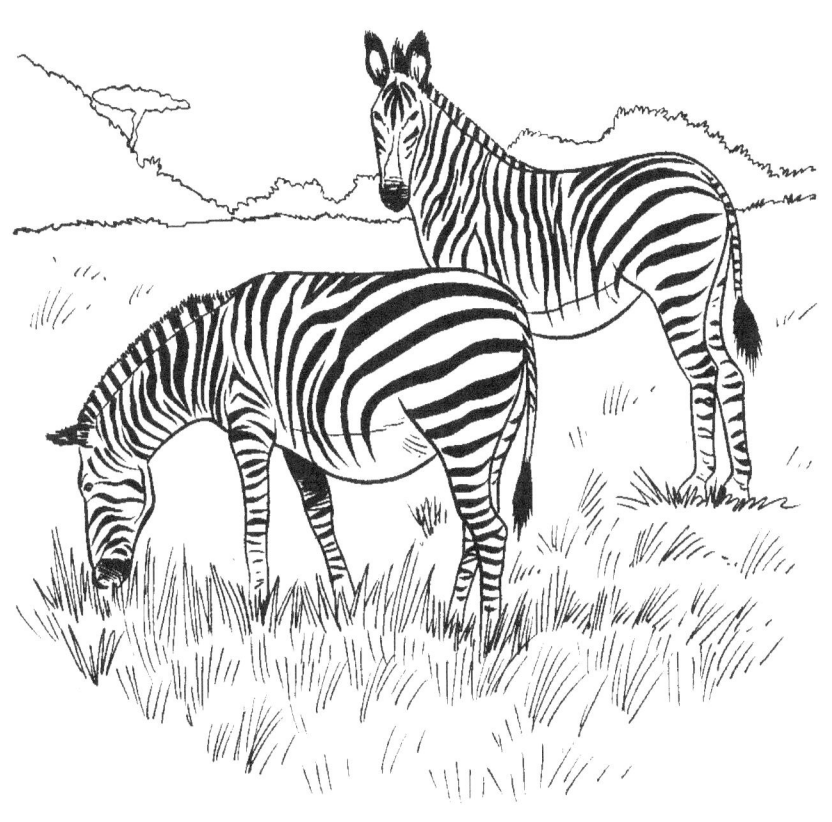

No two stripe coats on zebras are the same – just like our fingerprints!

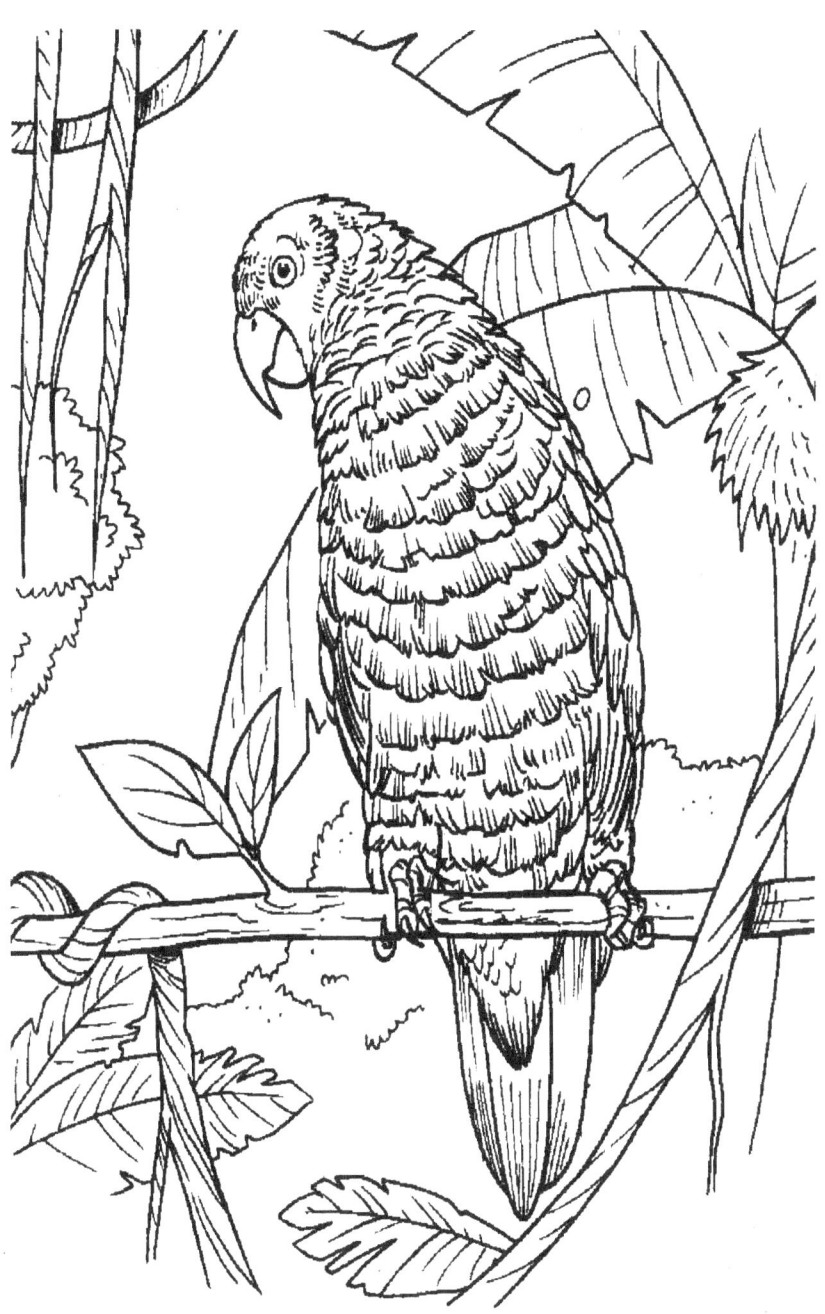

Parrot

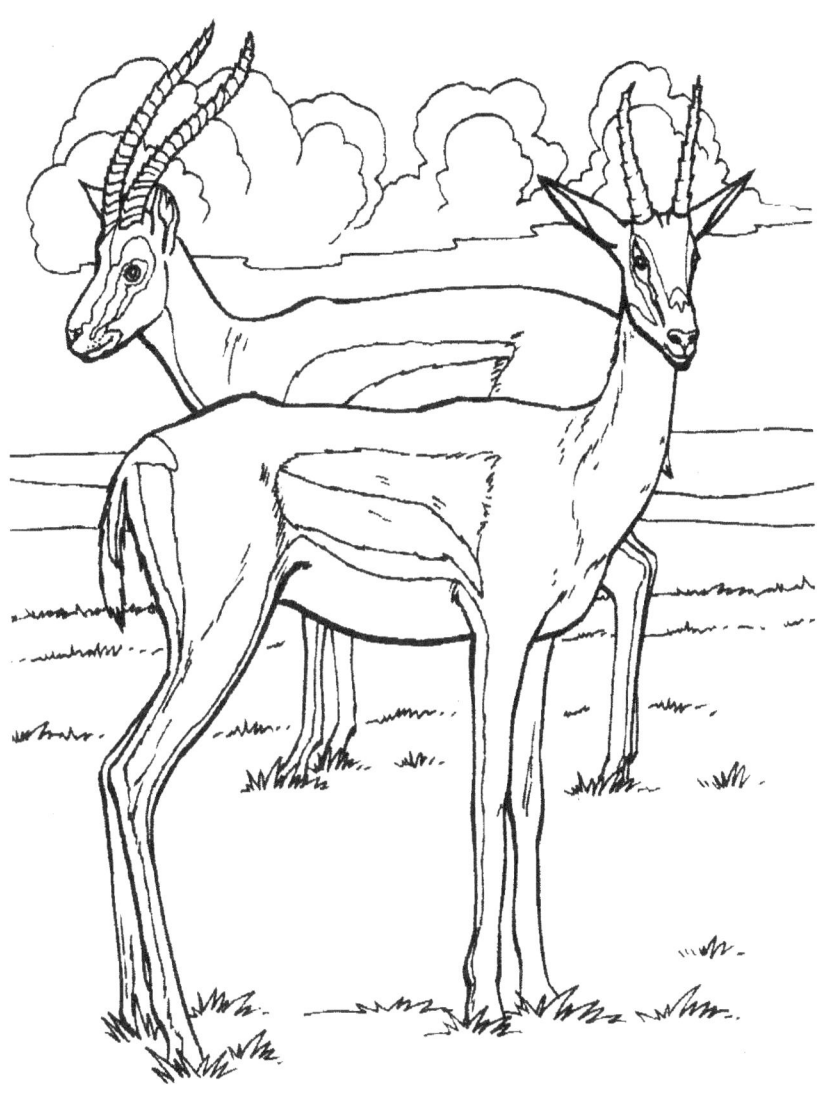

Gazelles

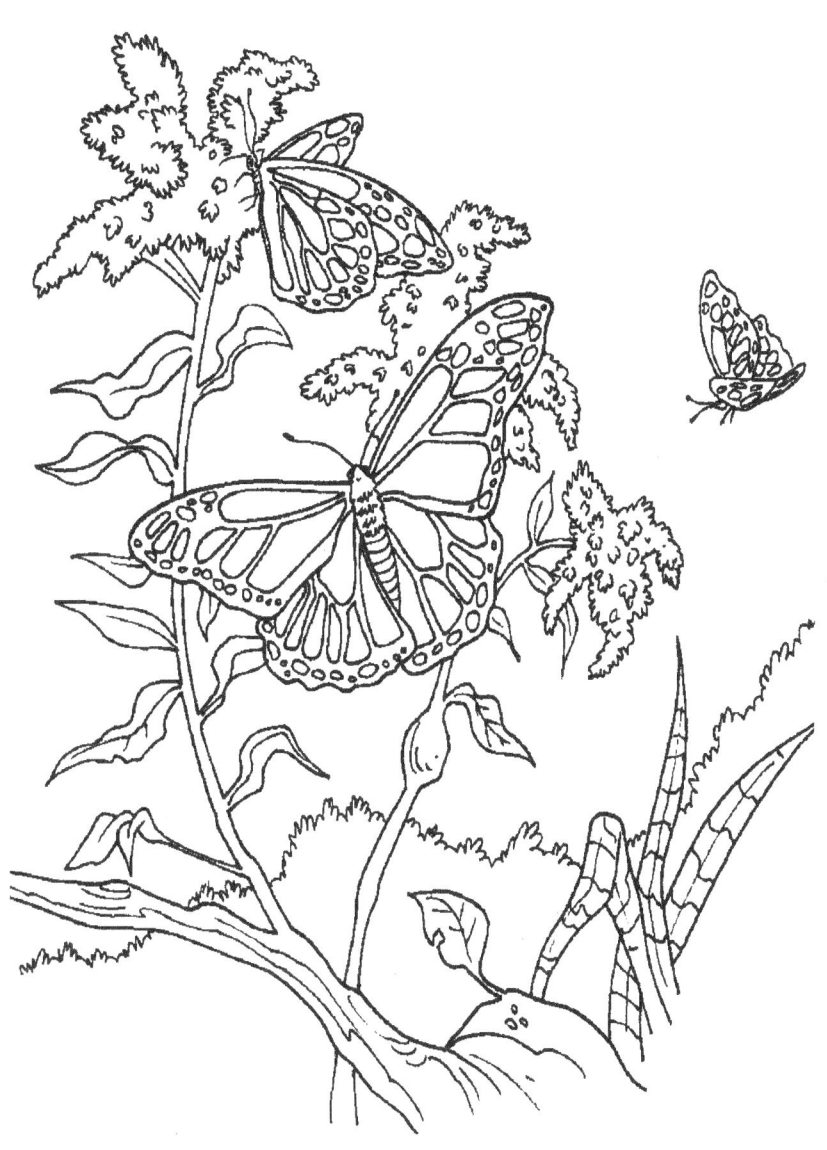

Butterflies

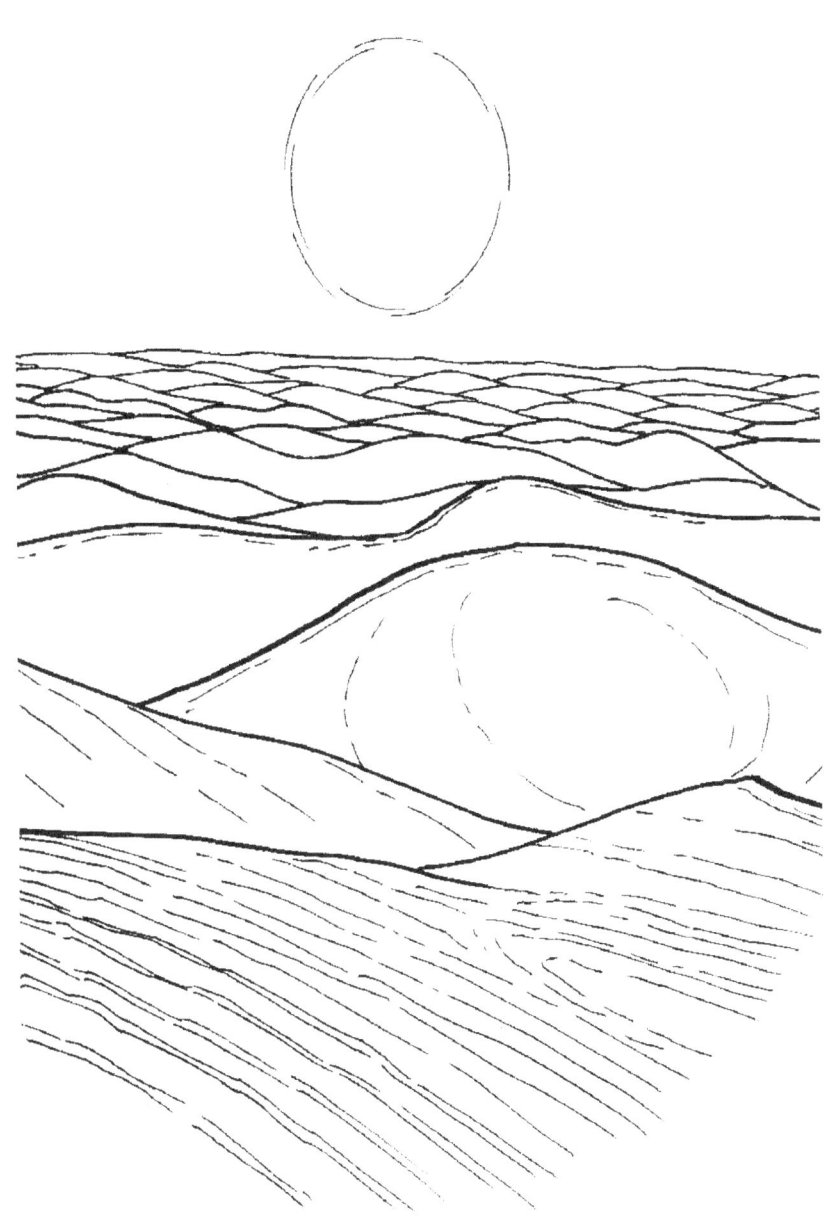

Sand Dunes

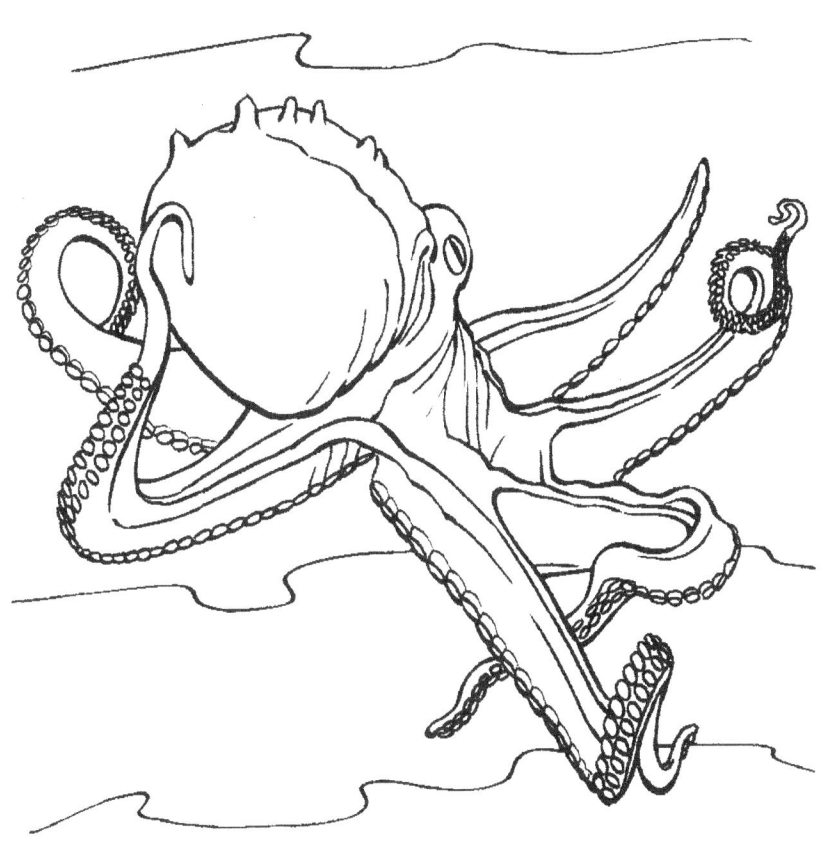

There are 200 species of octopus in the world.

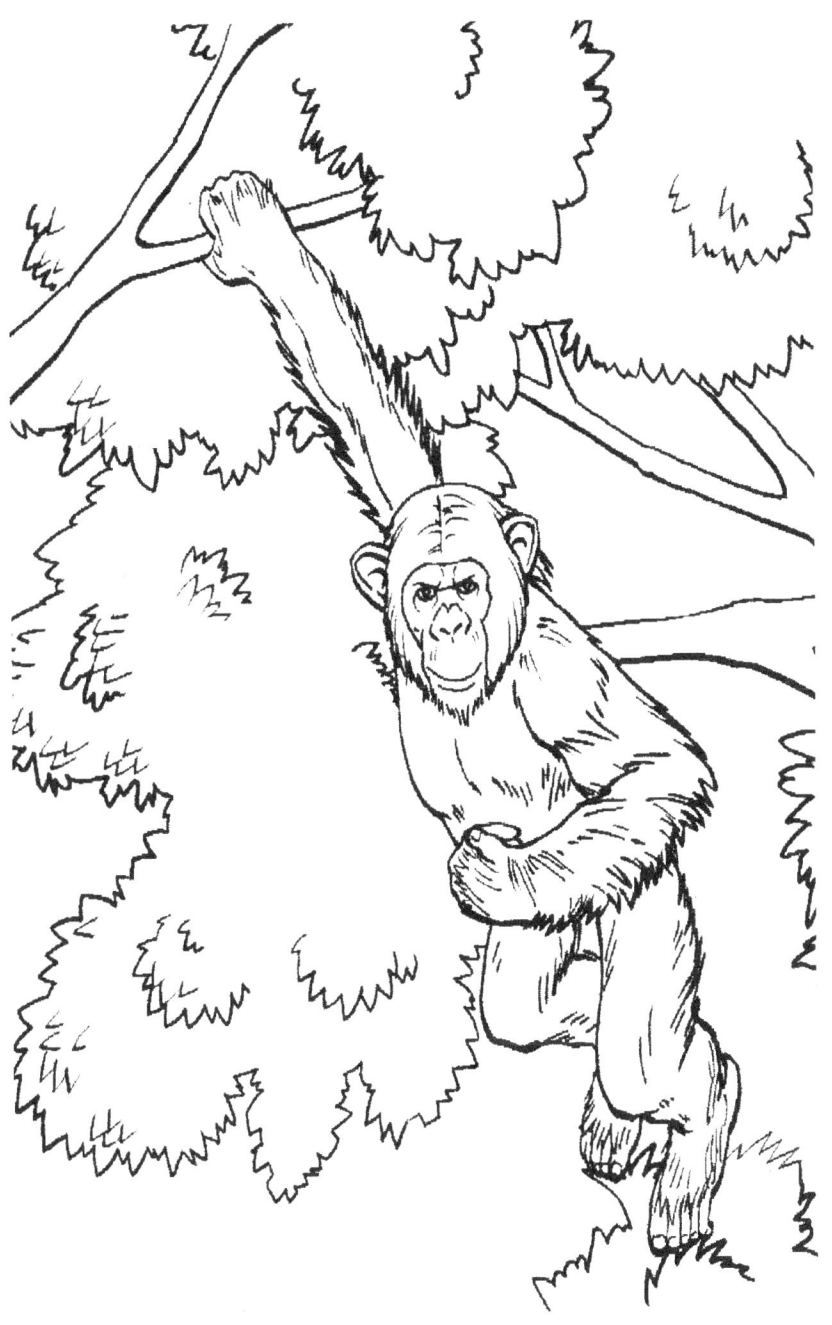

Chimpanzee

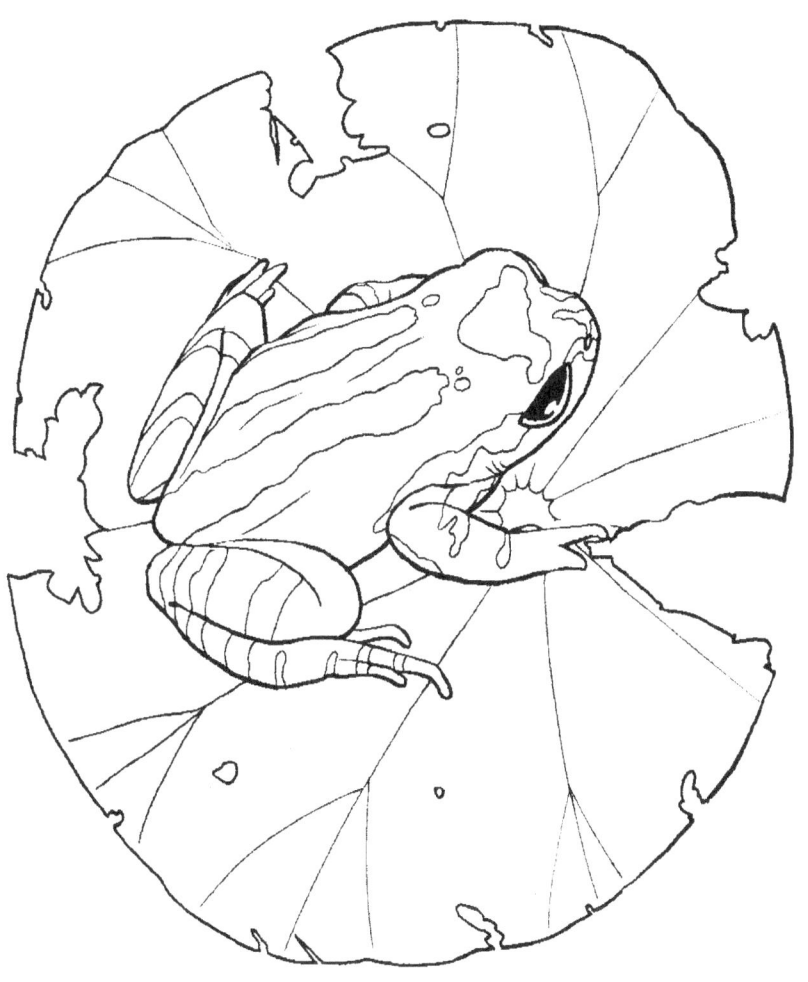

Frog

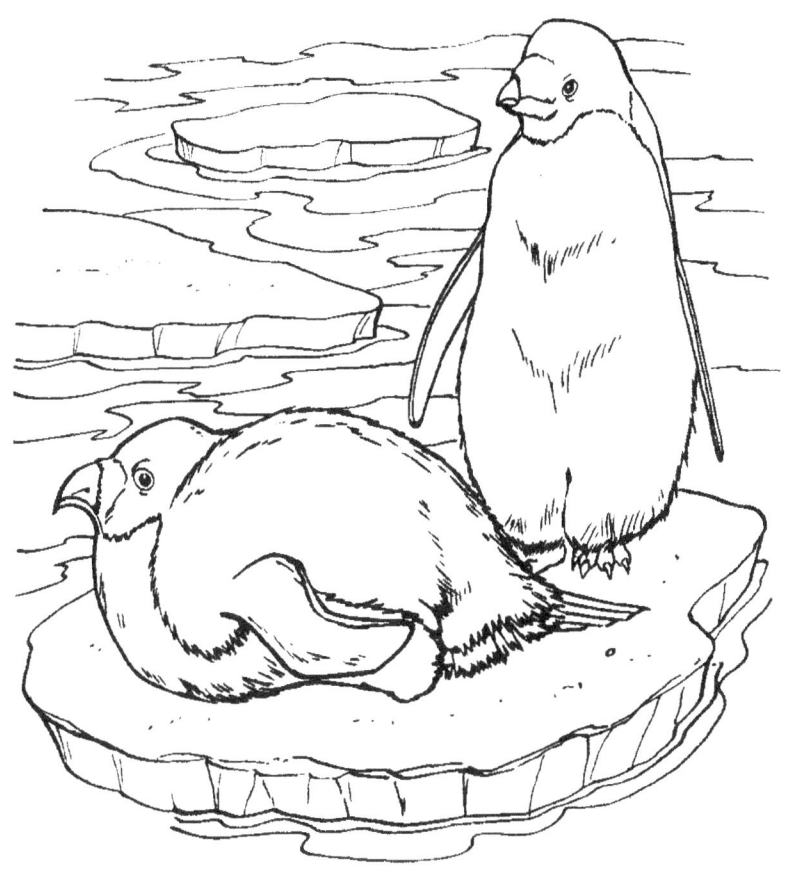

Penguins

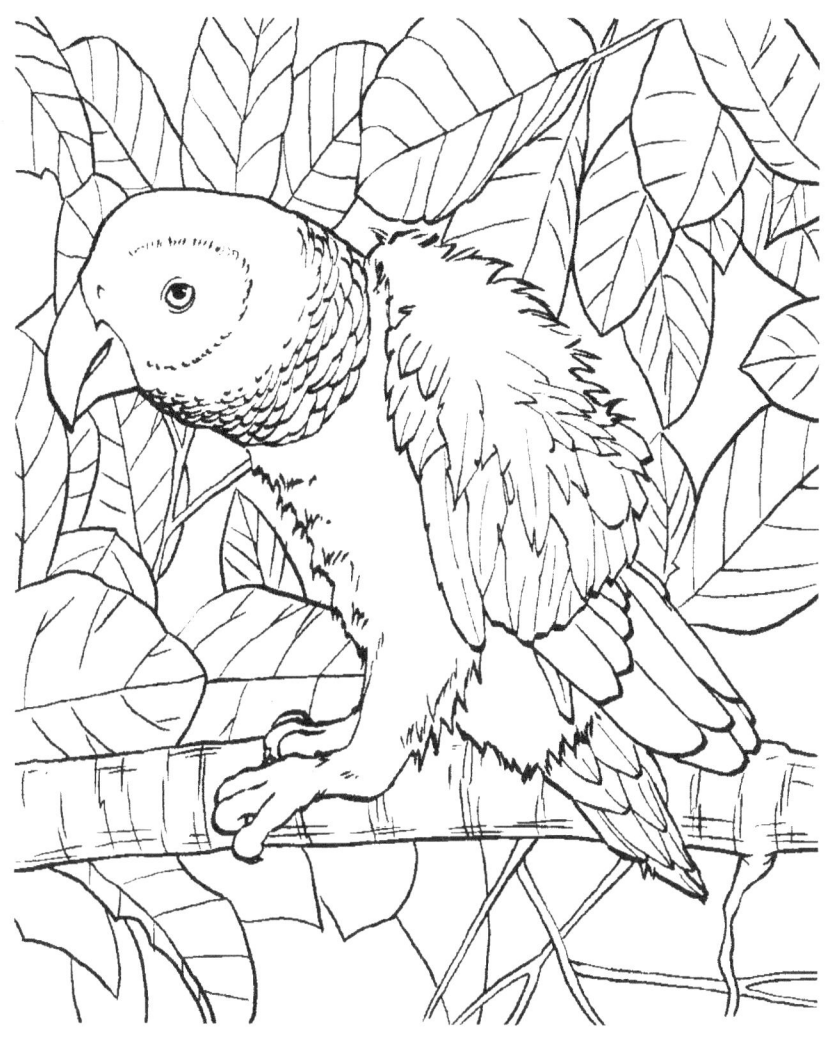

Parrots are vocal birds and make "screaming" calls to communicate to each other.

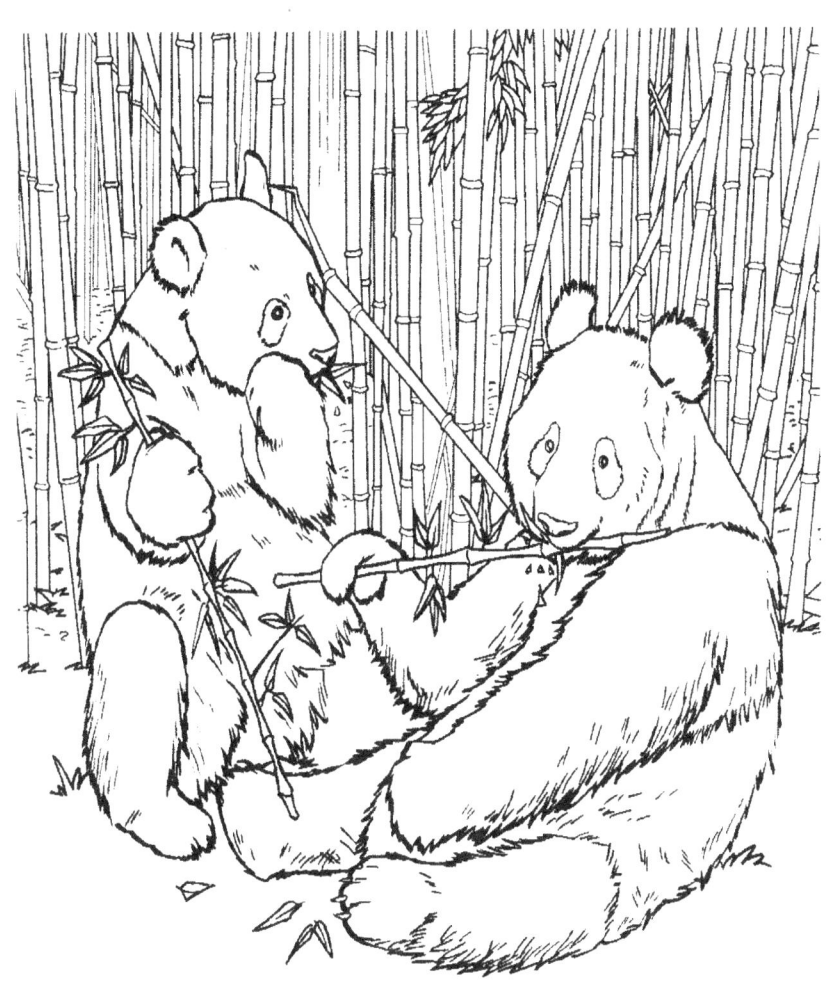

A giant panda eats up to 88 pounds of bamboo a day.

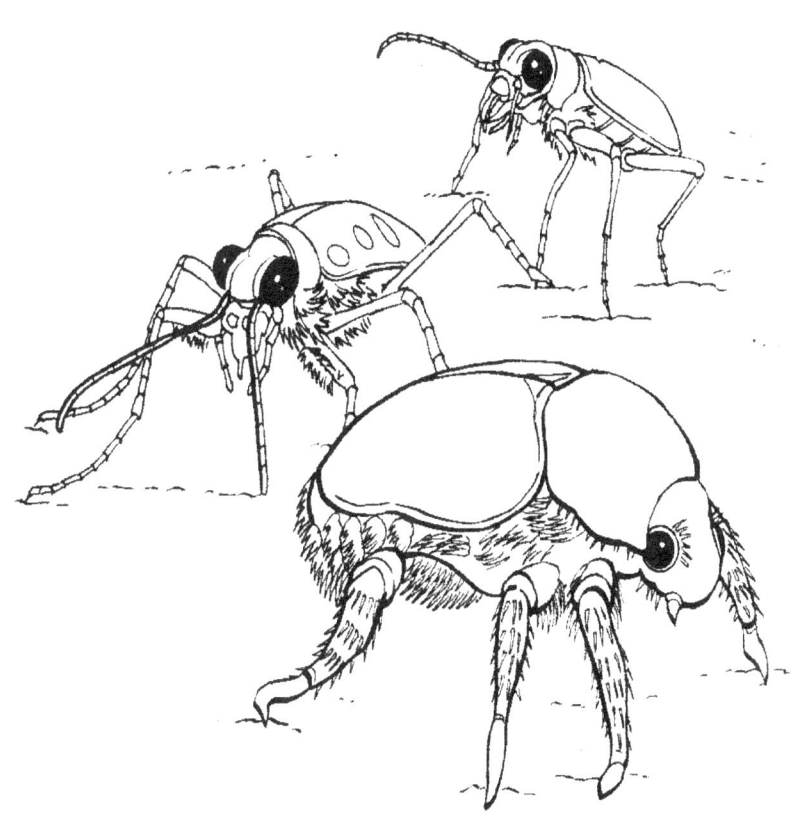

Beetles

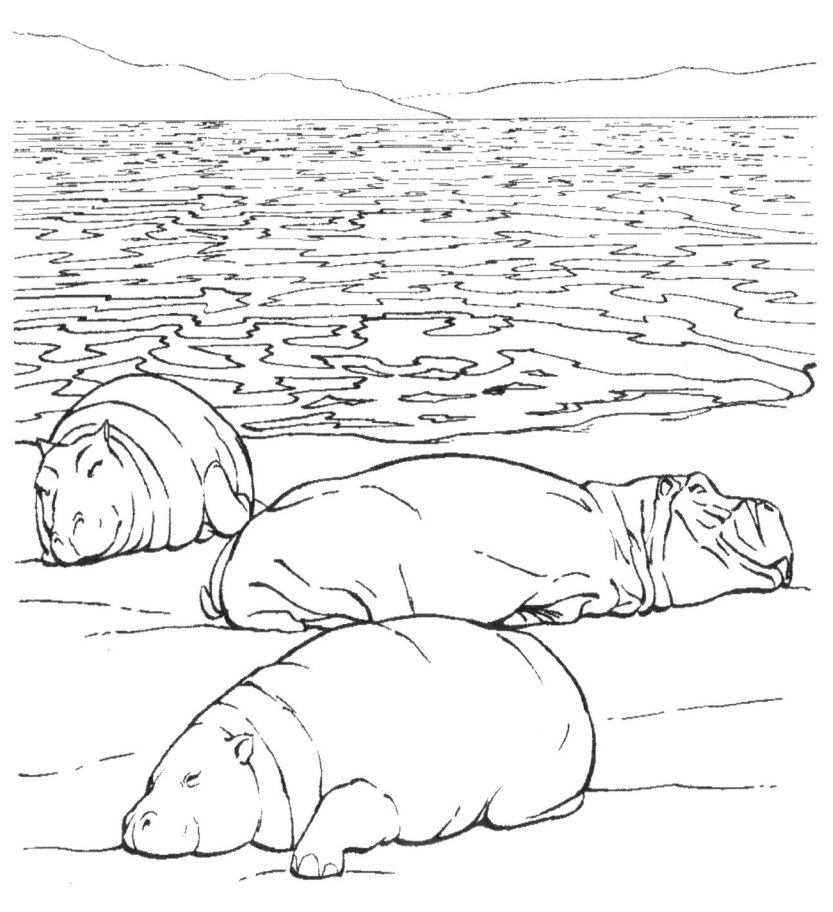

There are 2 species of hippo, both found in Africa.

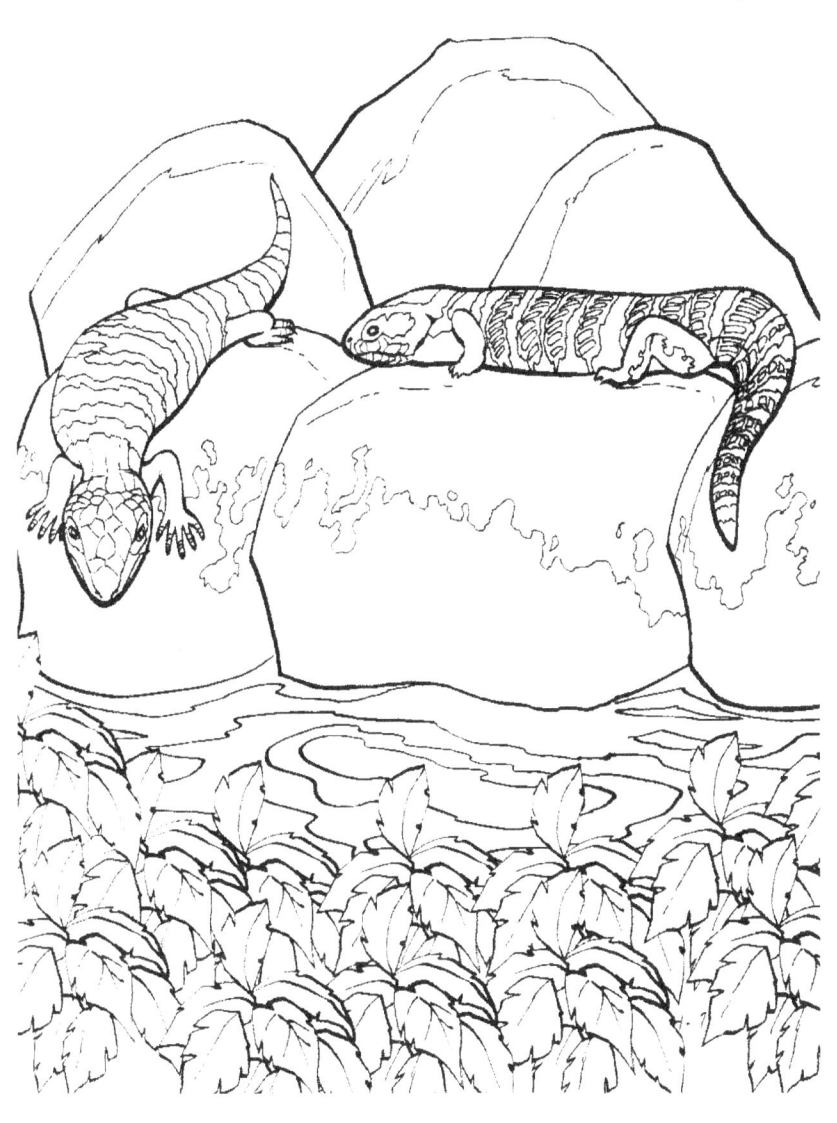

Common lizards remove the skin on their tails to fool predators.

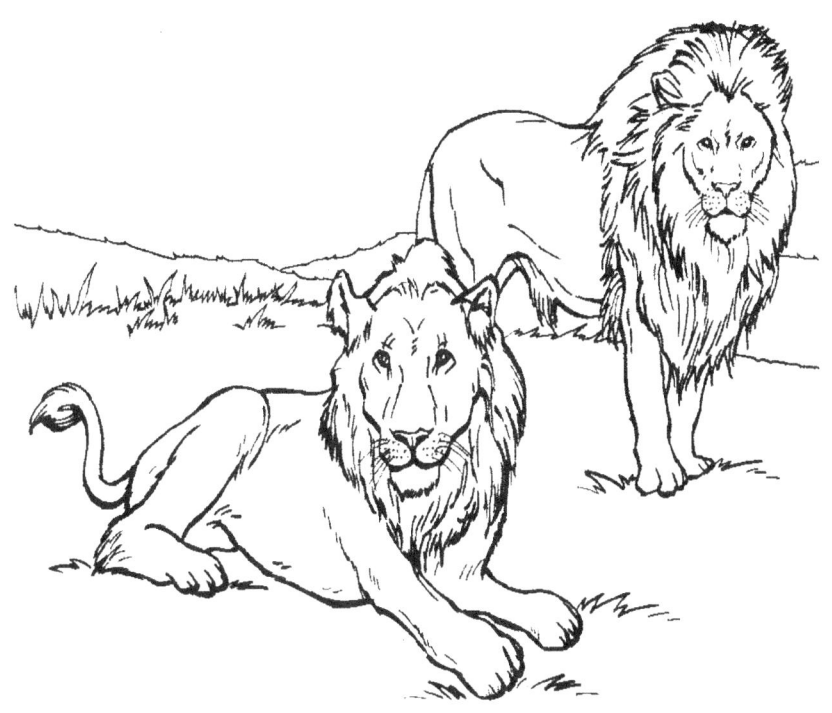

Lions

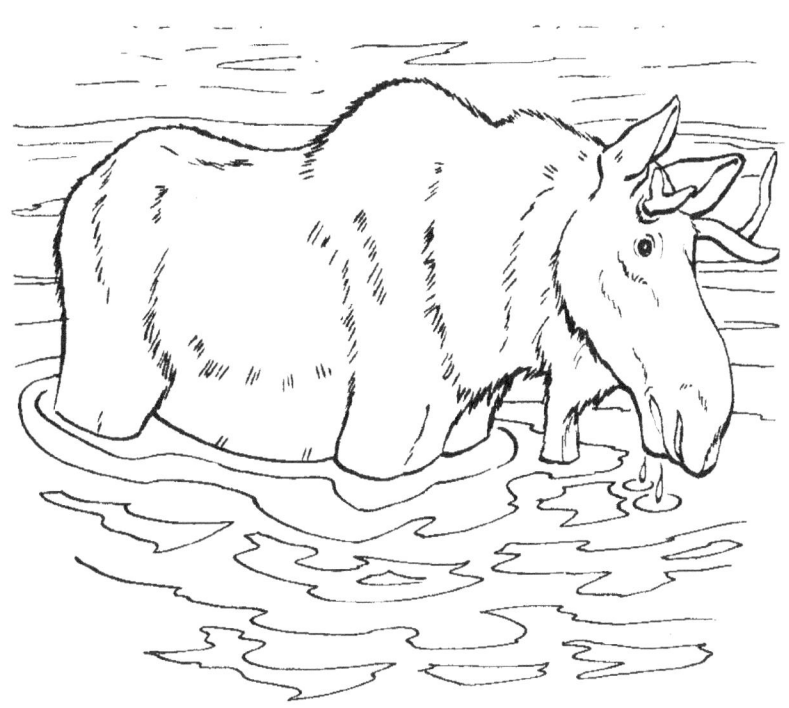

Moose

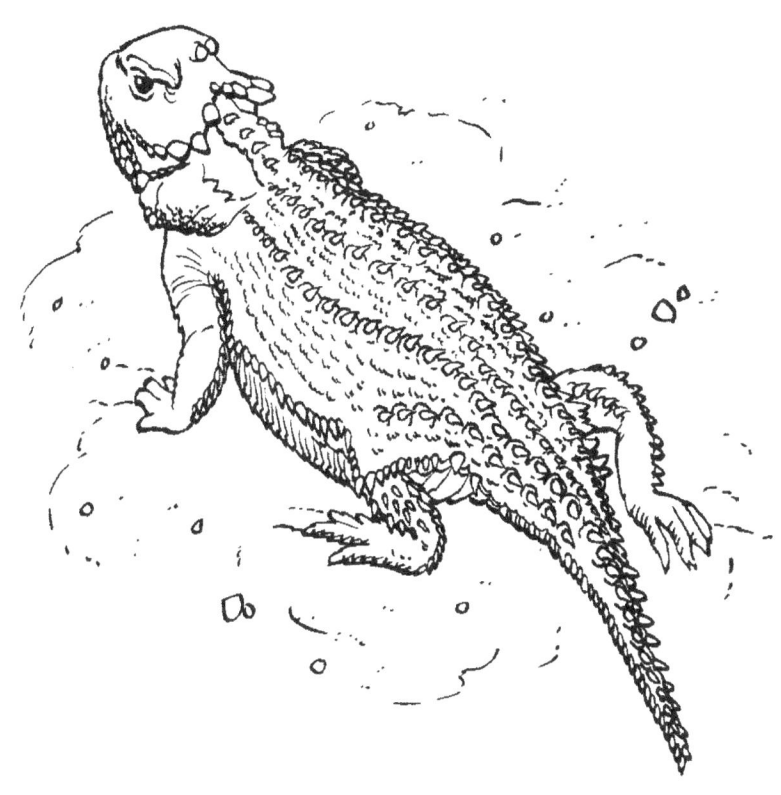

Lizard

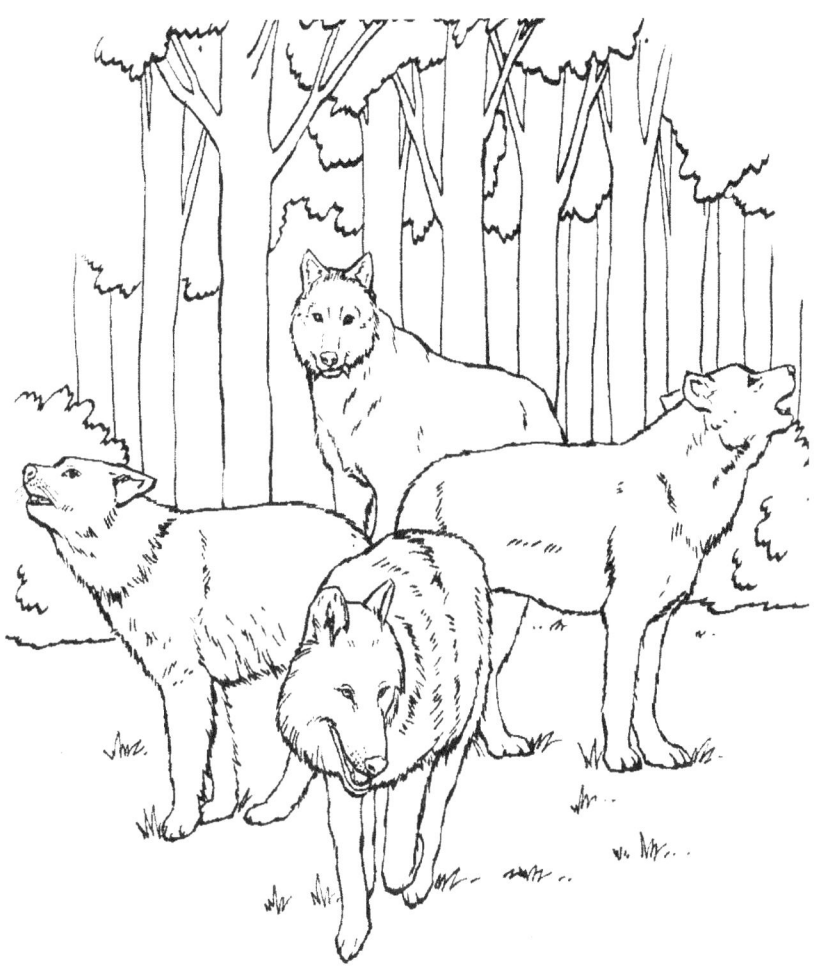

Wolves

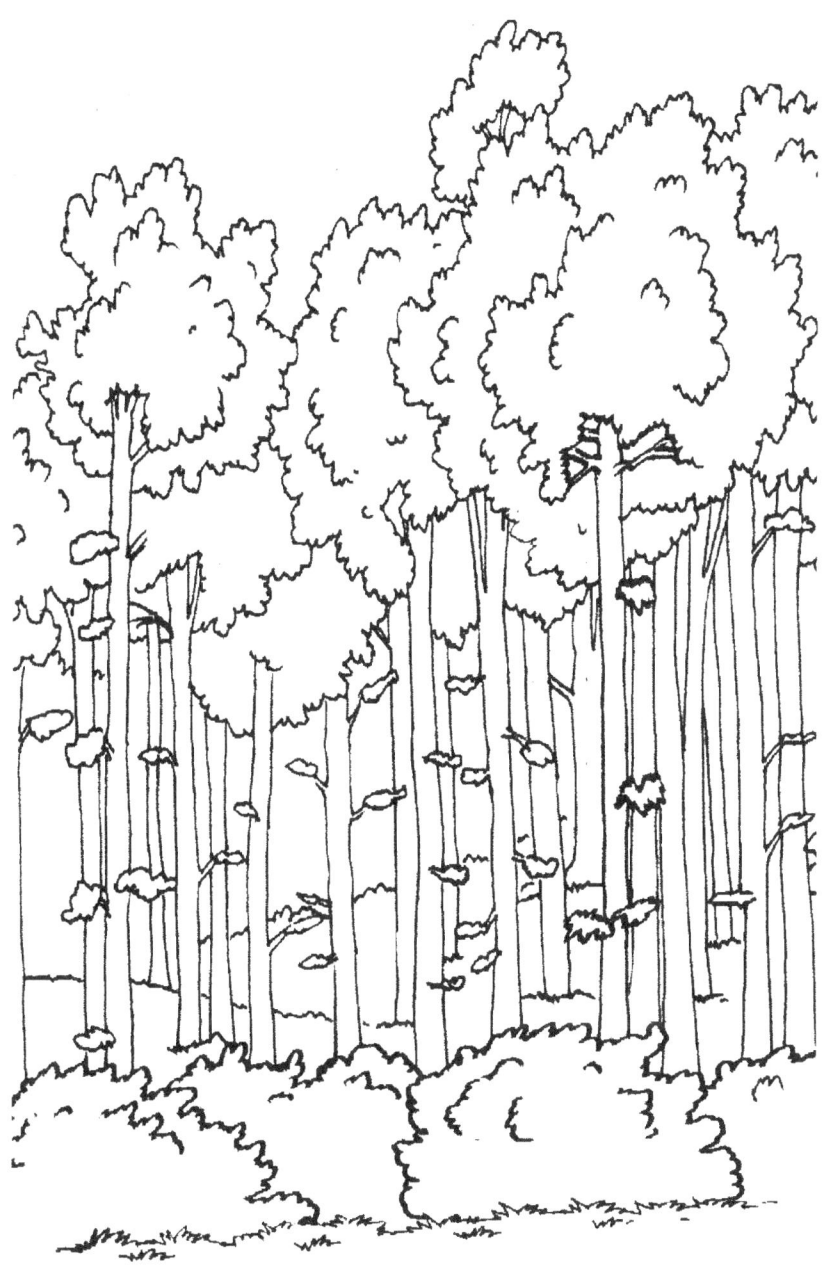

Forests cover 1/3 of the Earth's surface.

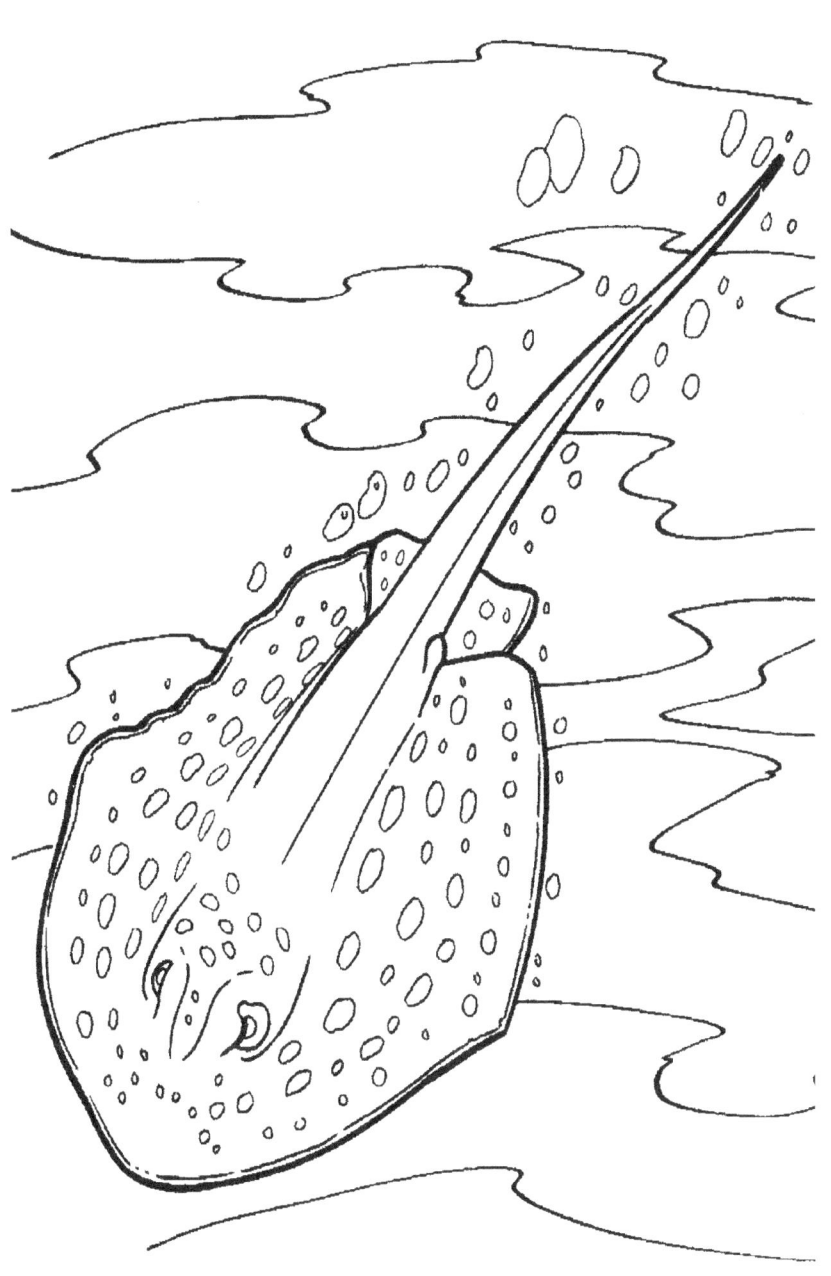

Stingray

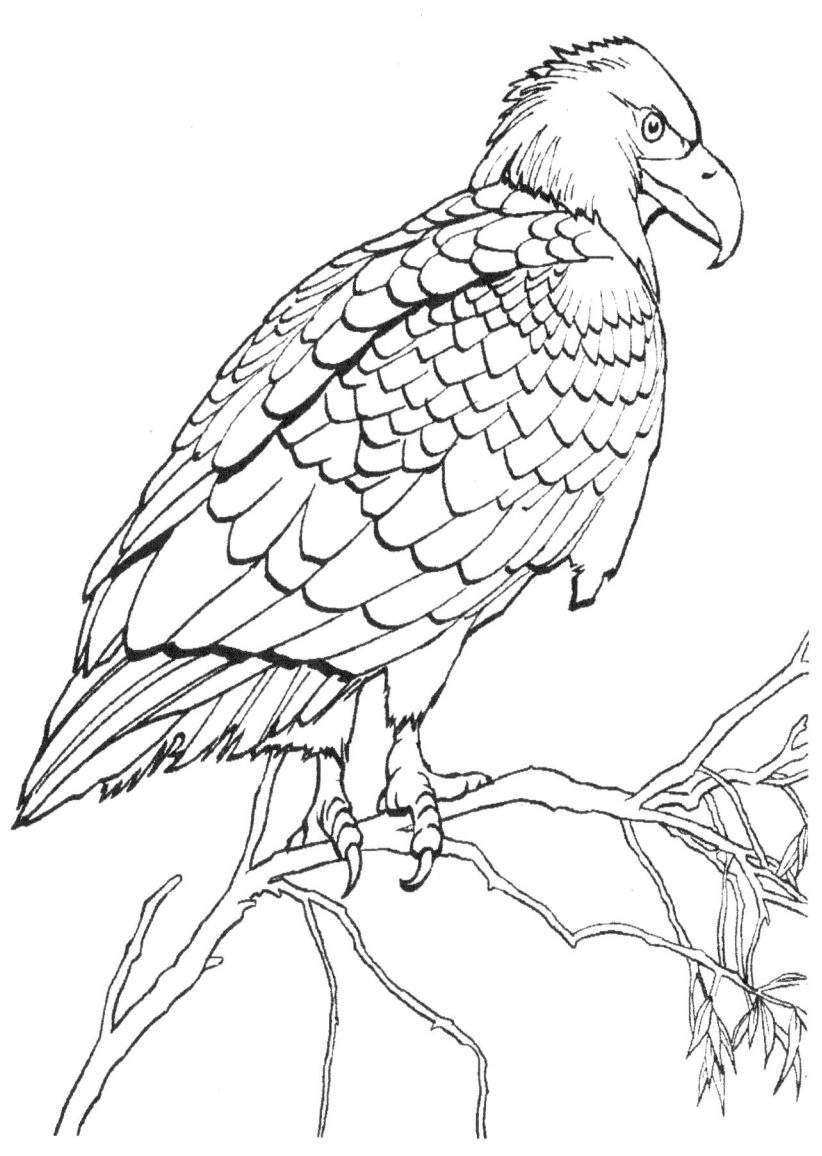

Eagles are the most magnificent birds of prey.

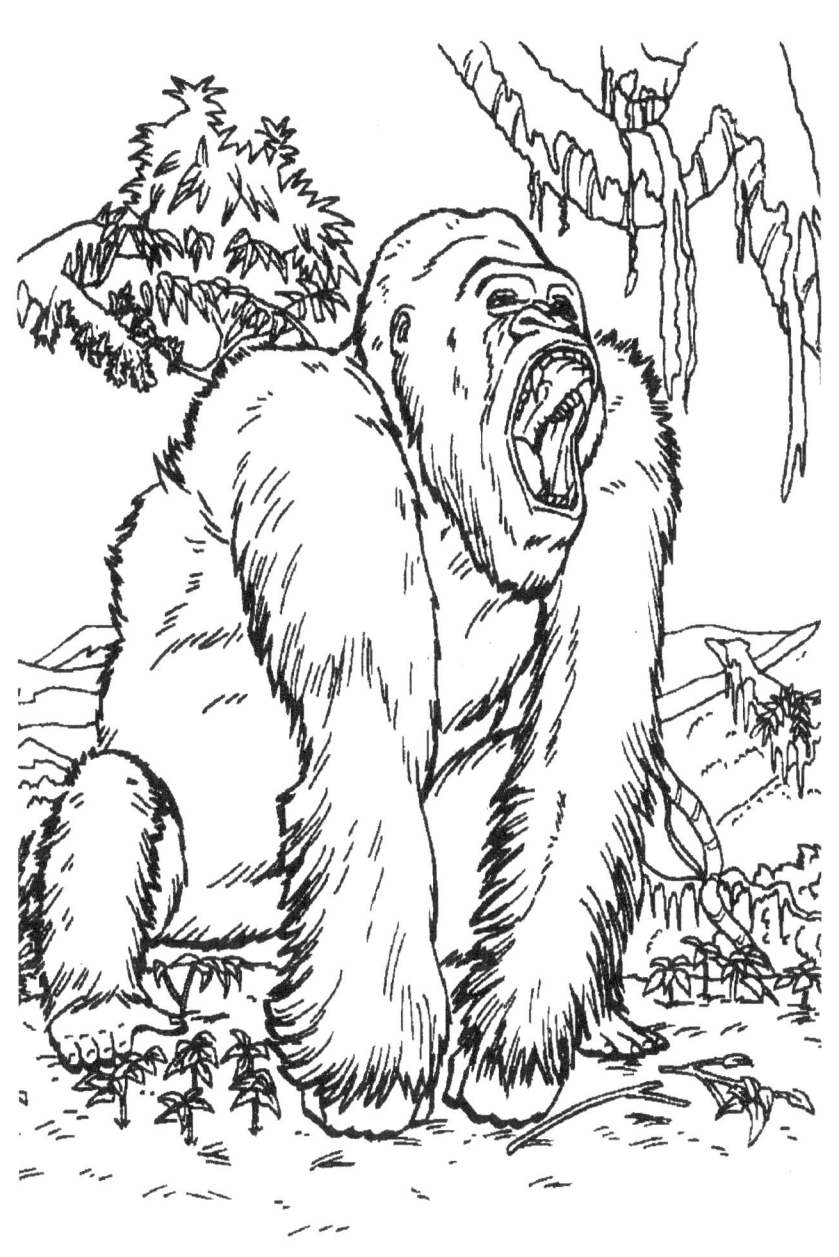

Gorilla

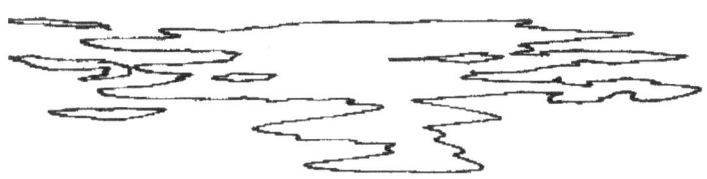

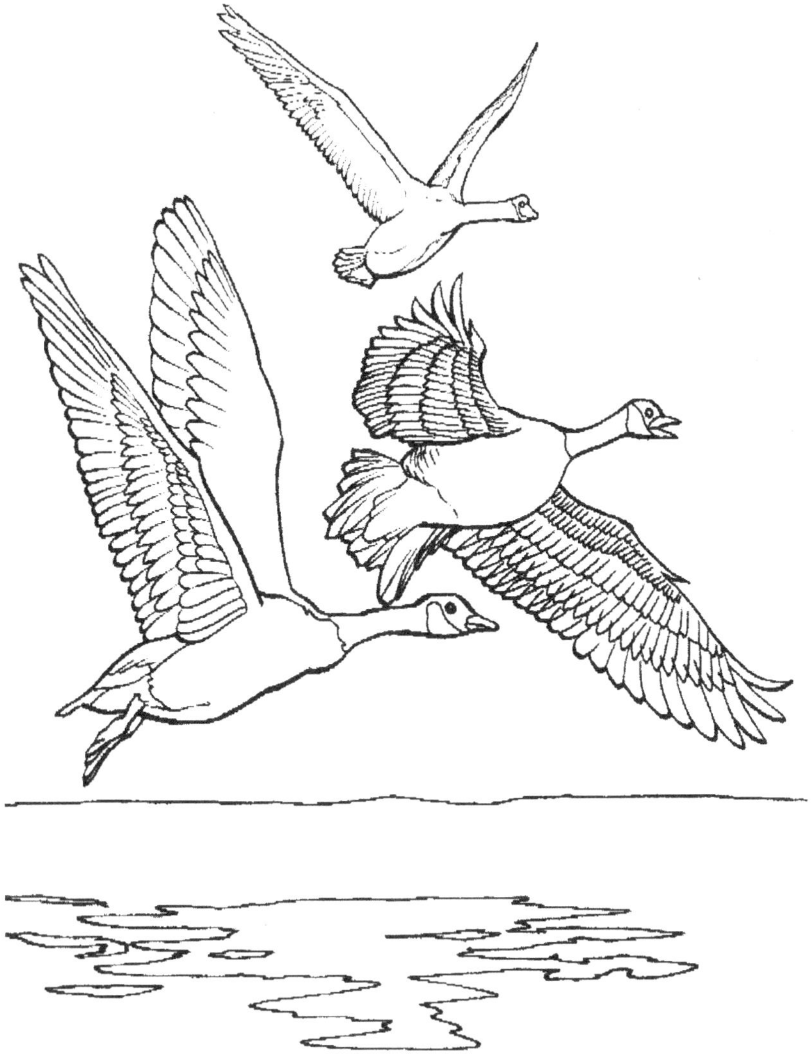

Geese

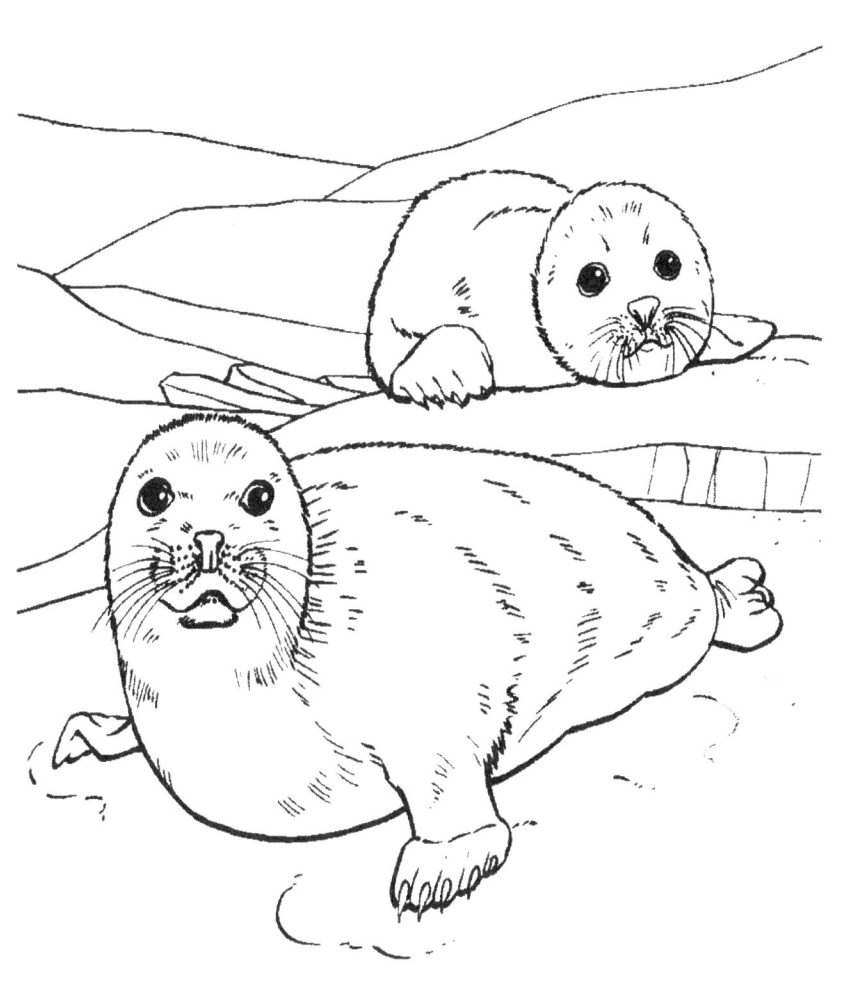

Seals

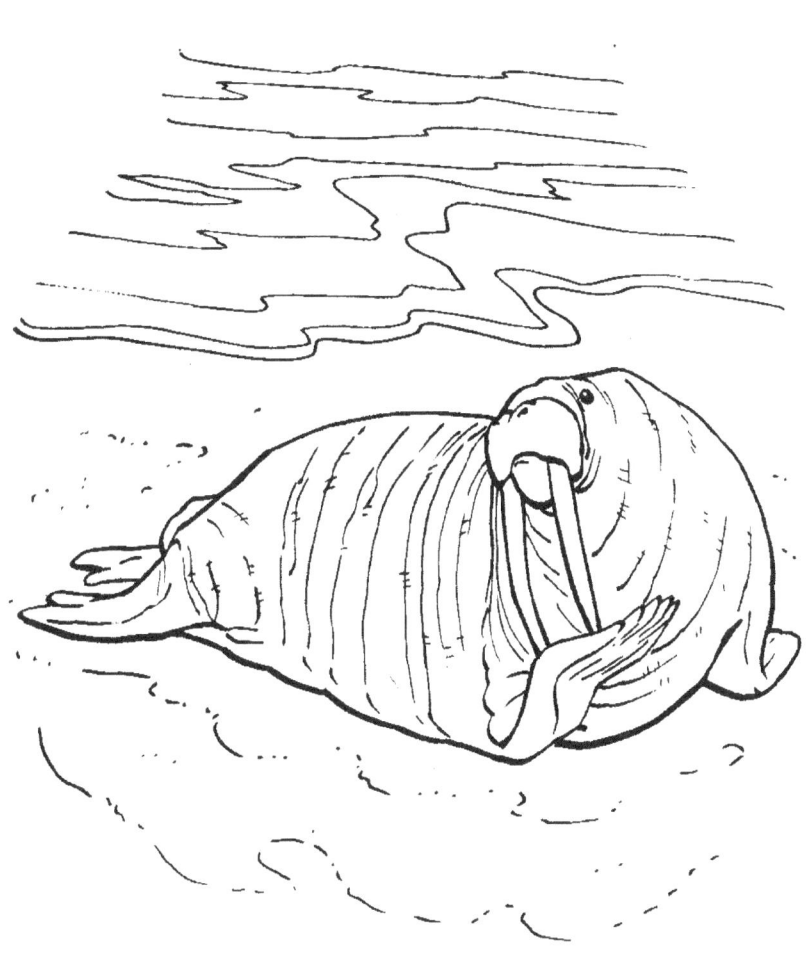

Walrus

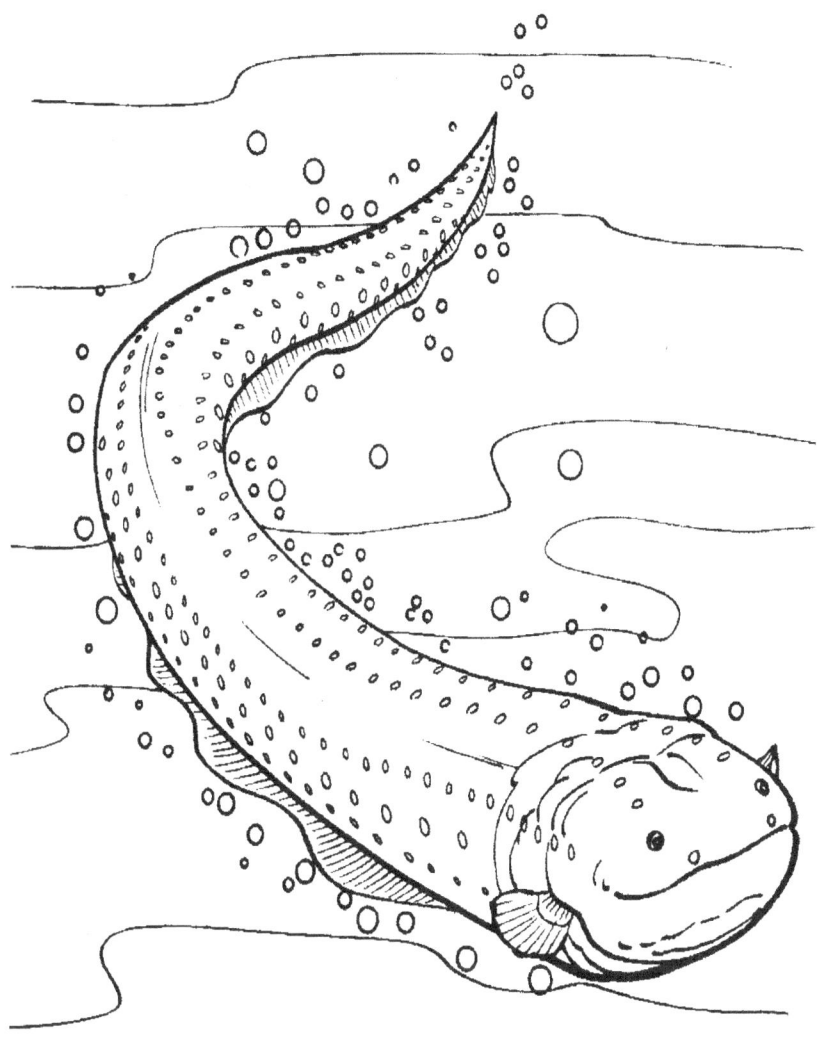

Electric Eel

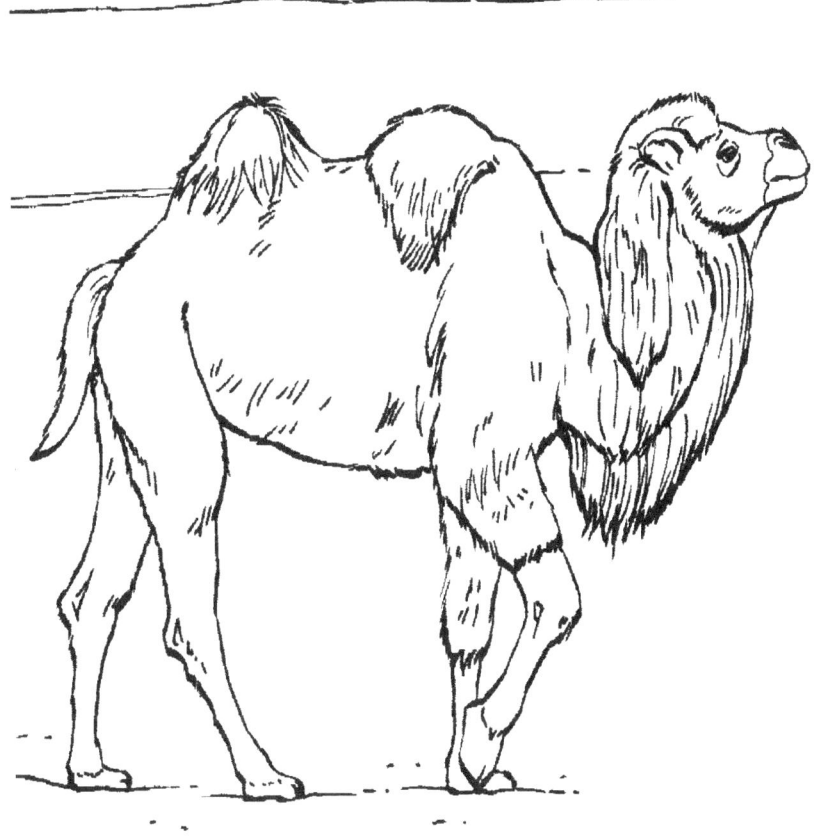

Camel

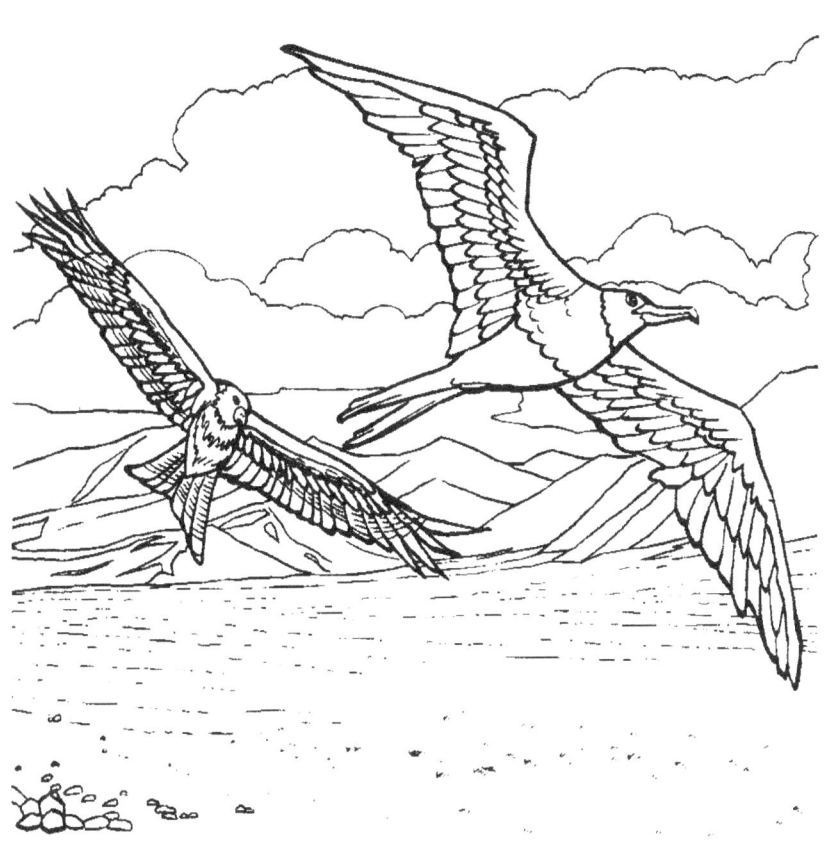

Sea Gulls

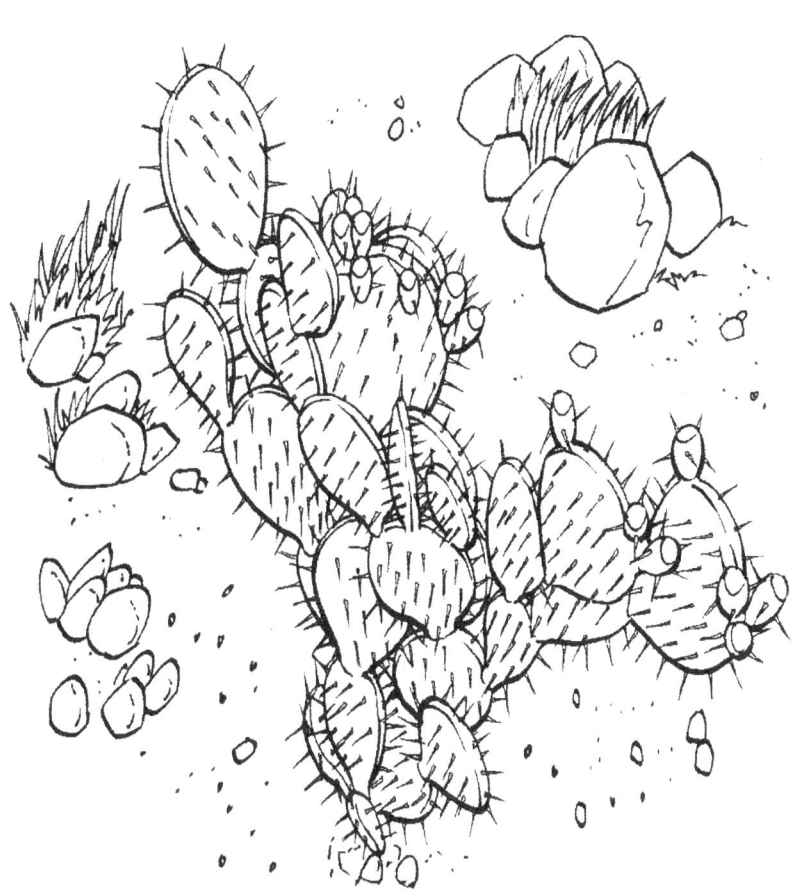

Cactus

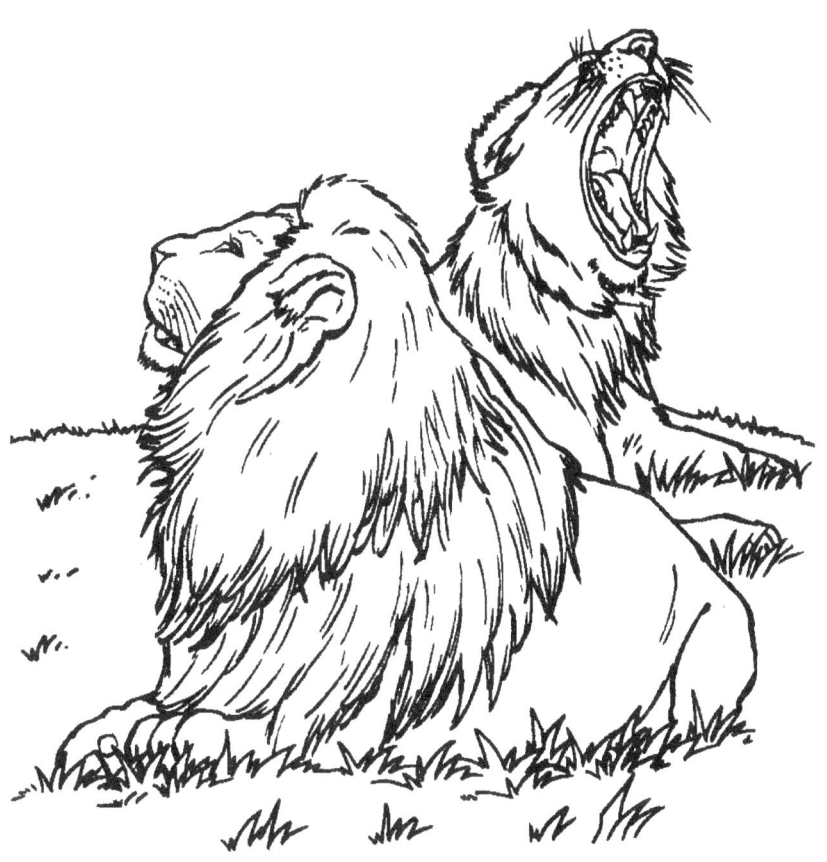

Lions

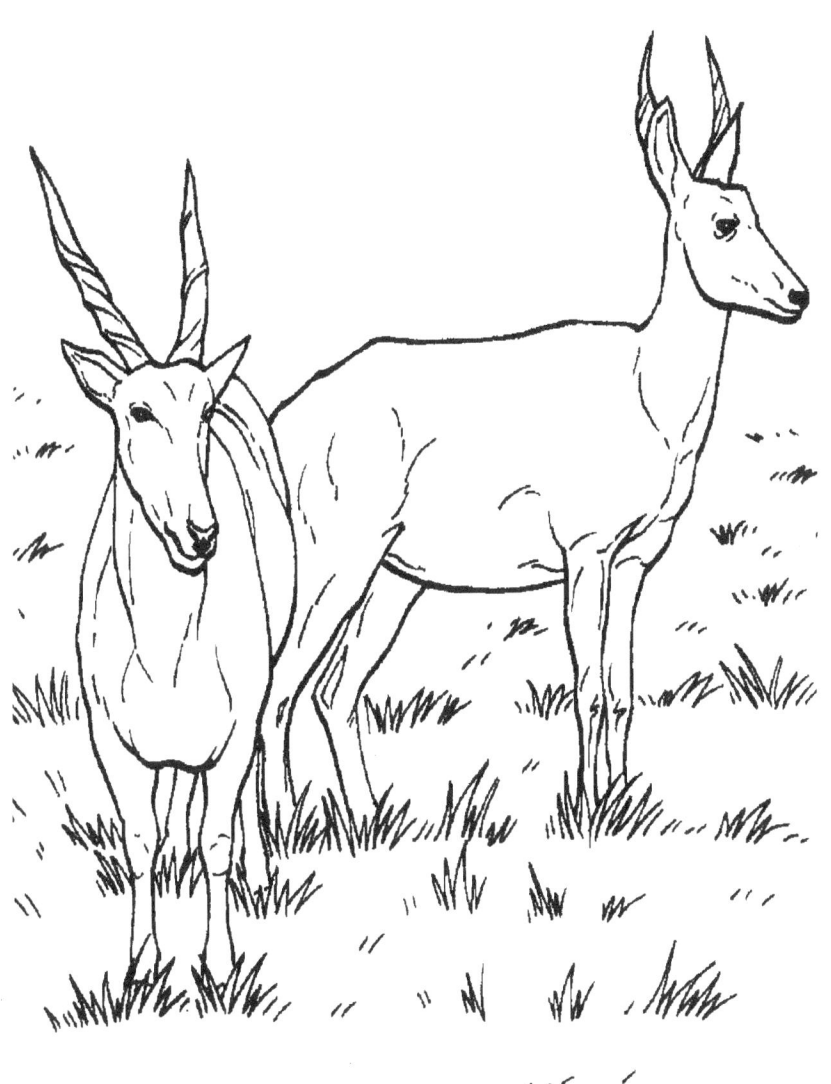

Antelopes

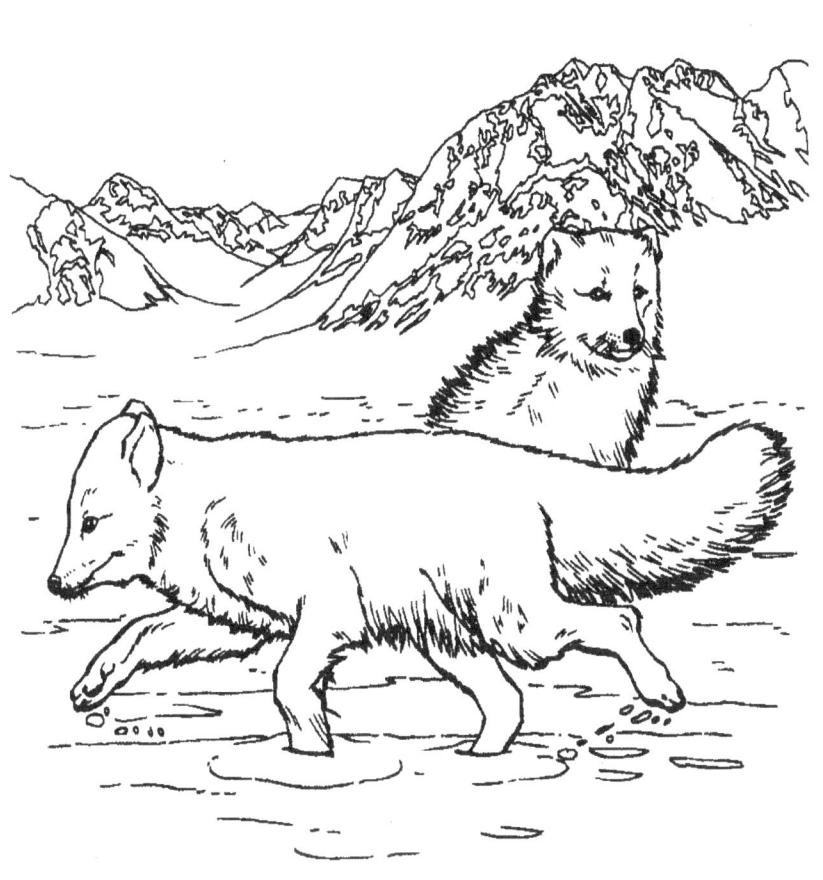

Arctic Foxes

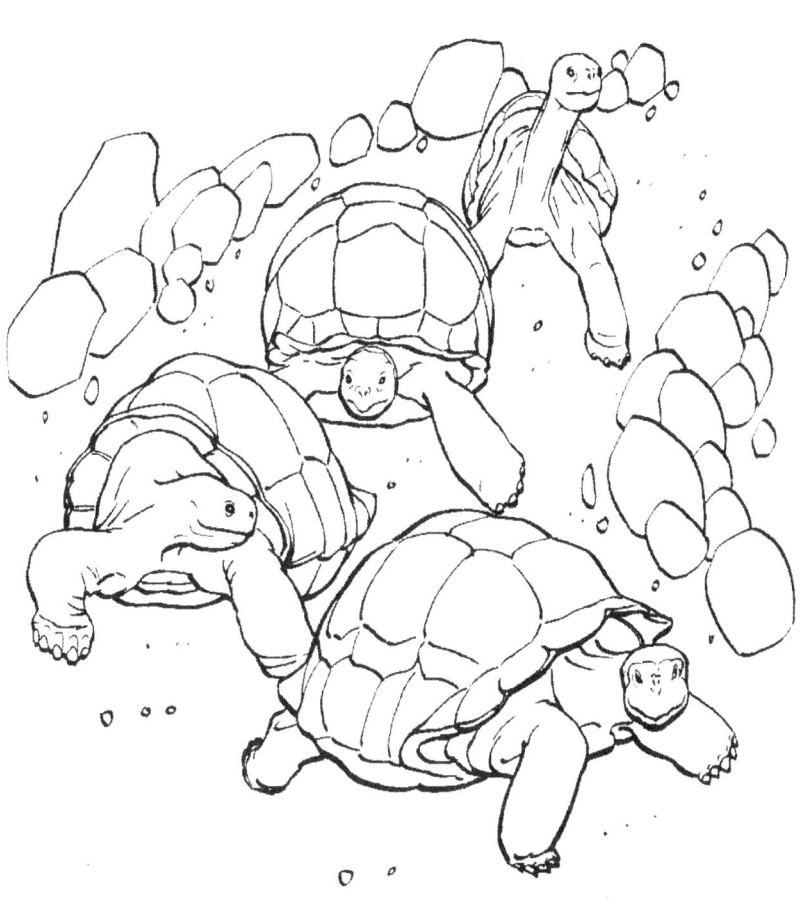

Tortoises

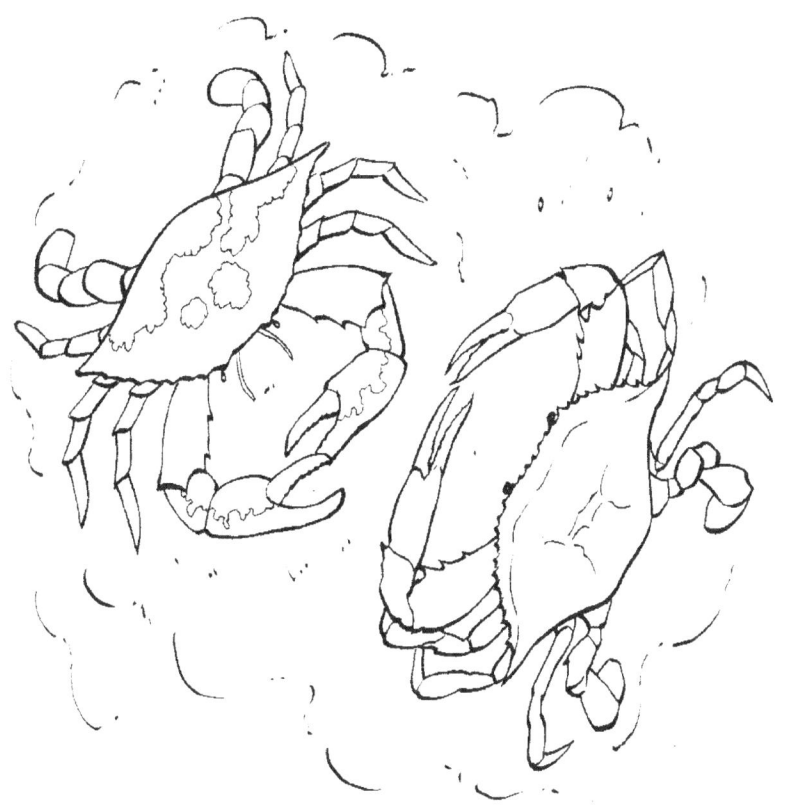

Crabs

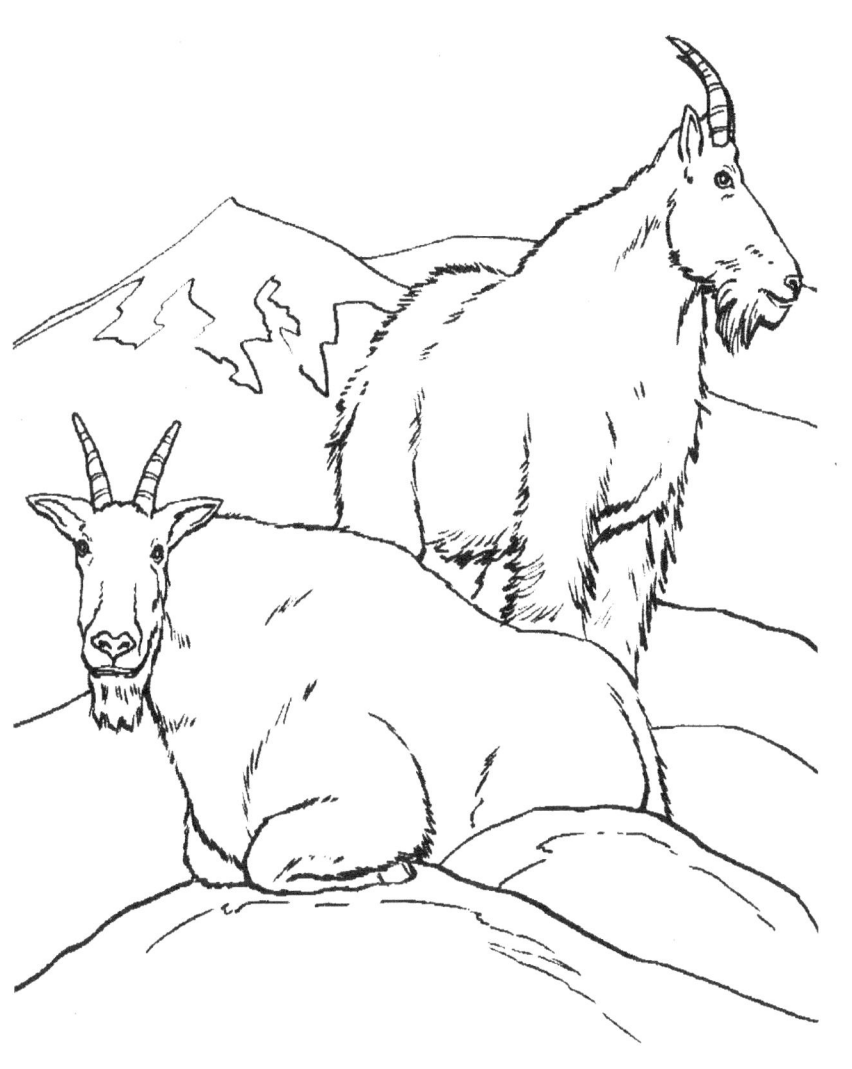

Mountain Goats

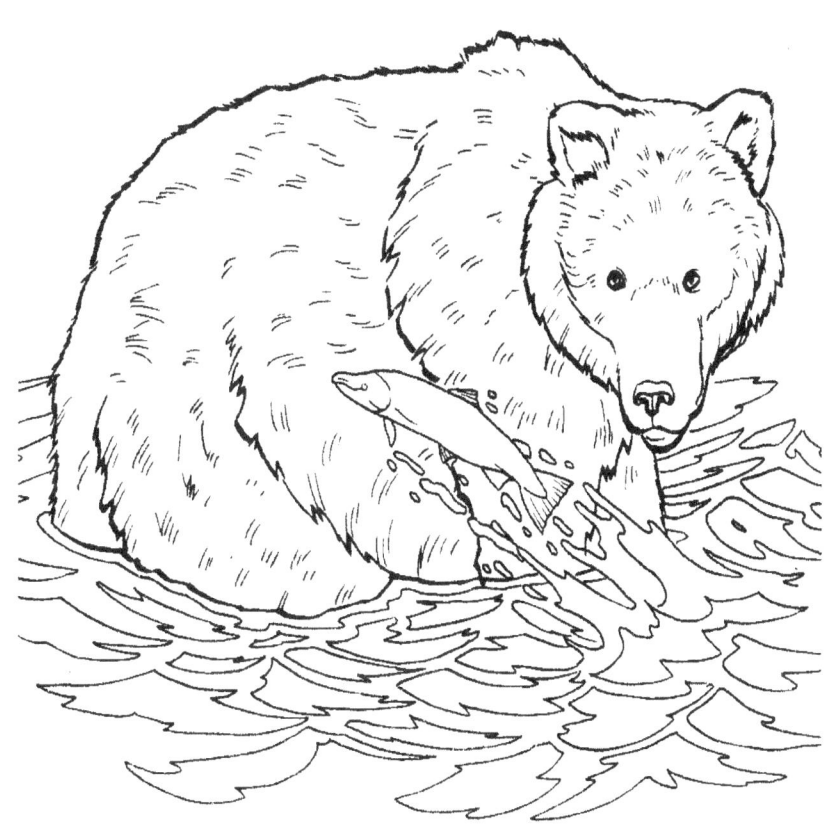

Grizzly Bear

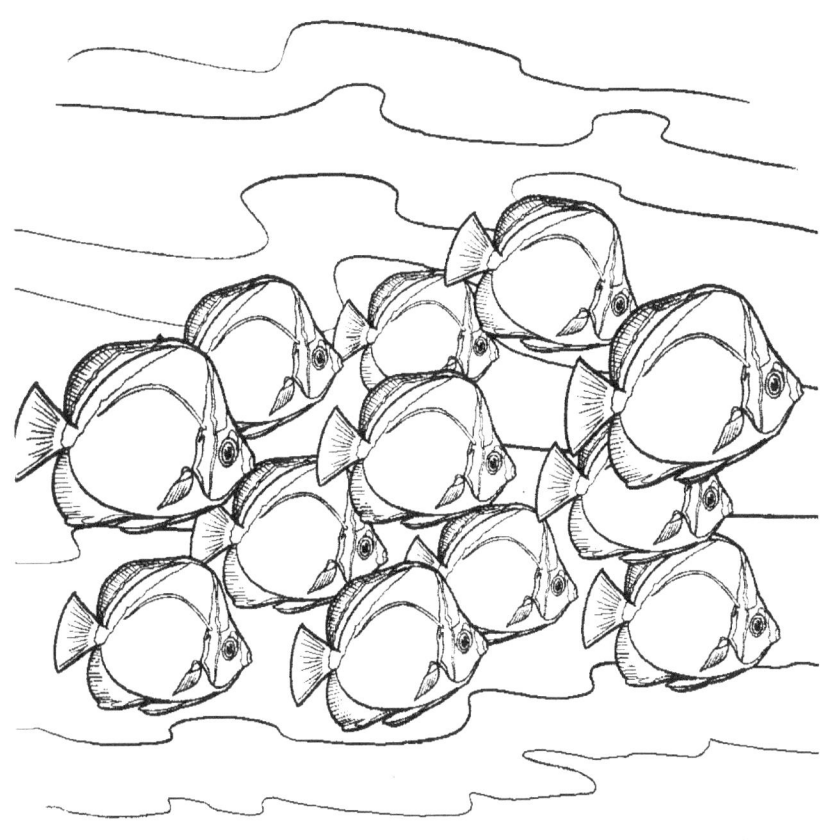

Fish

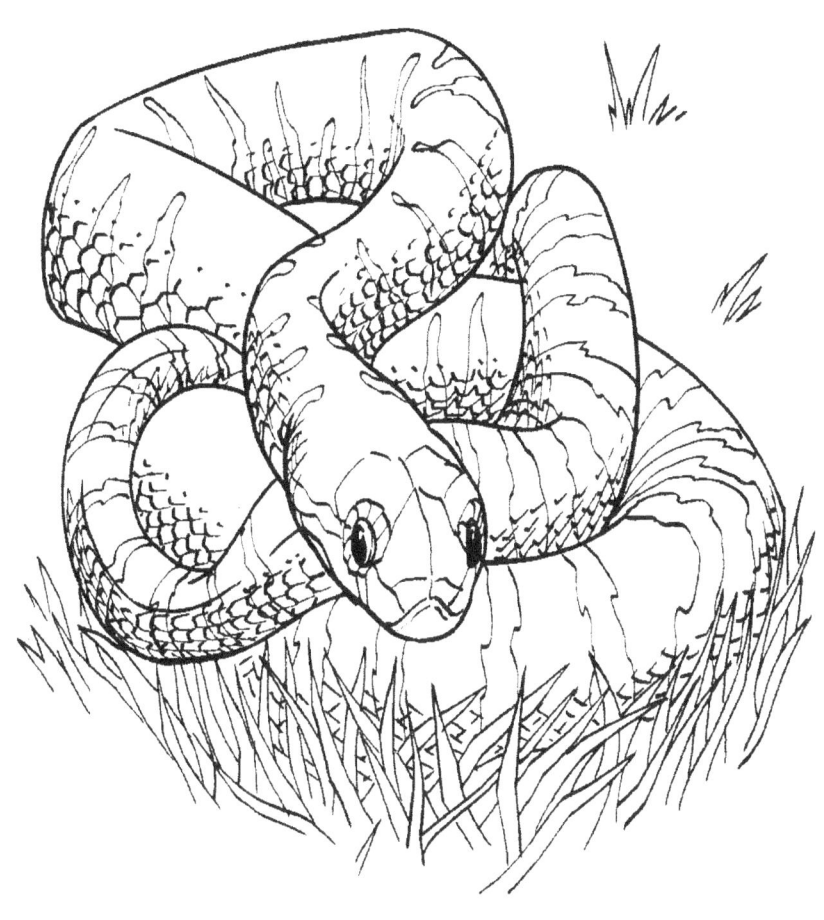

Anaconda

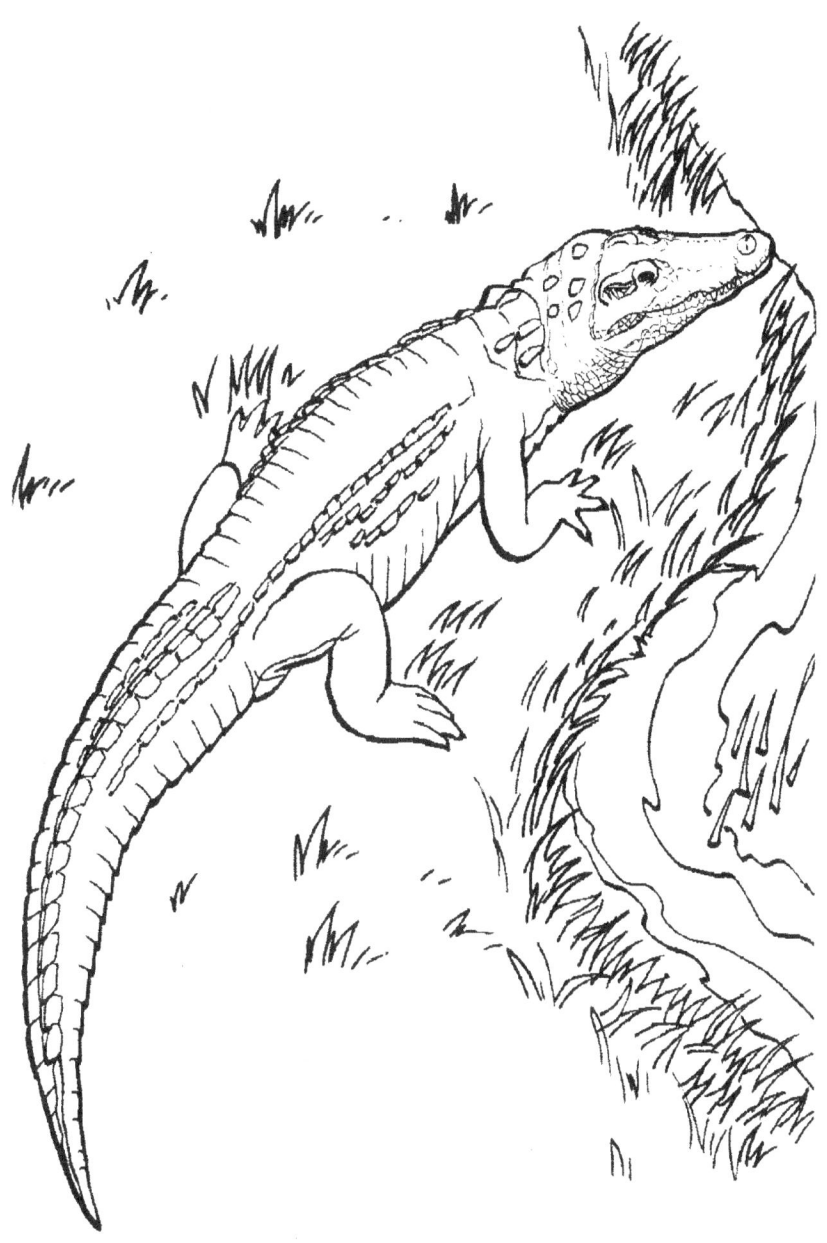

Crocodile

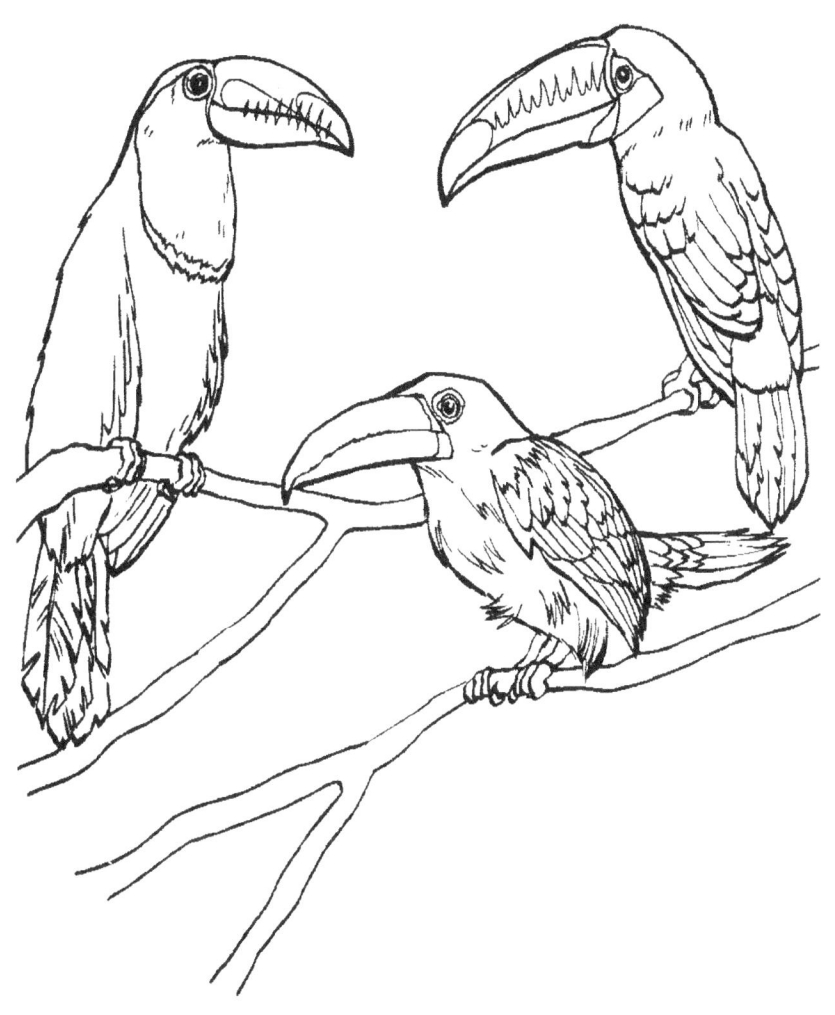

The toucan's most prominent feature is its bill.

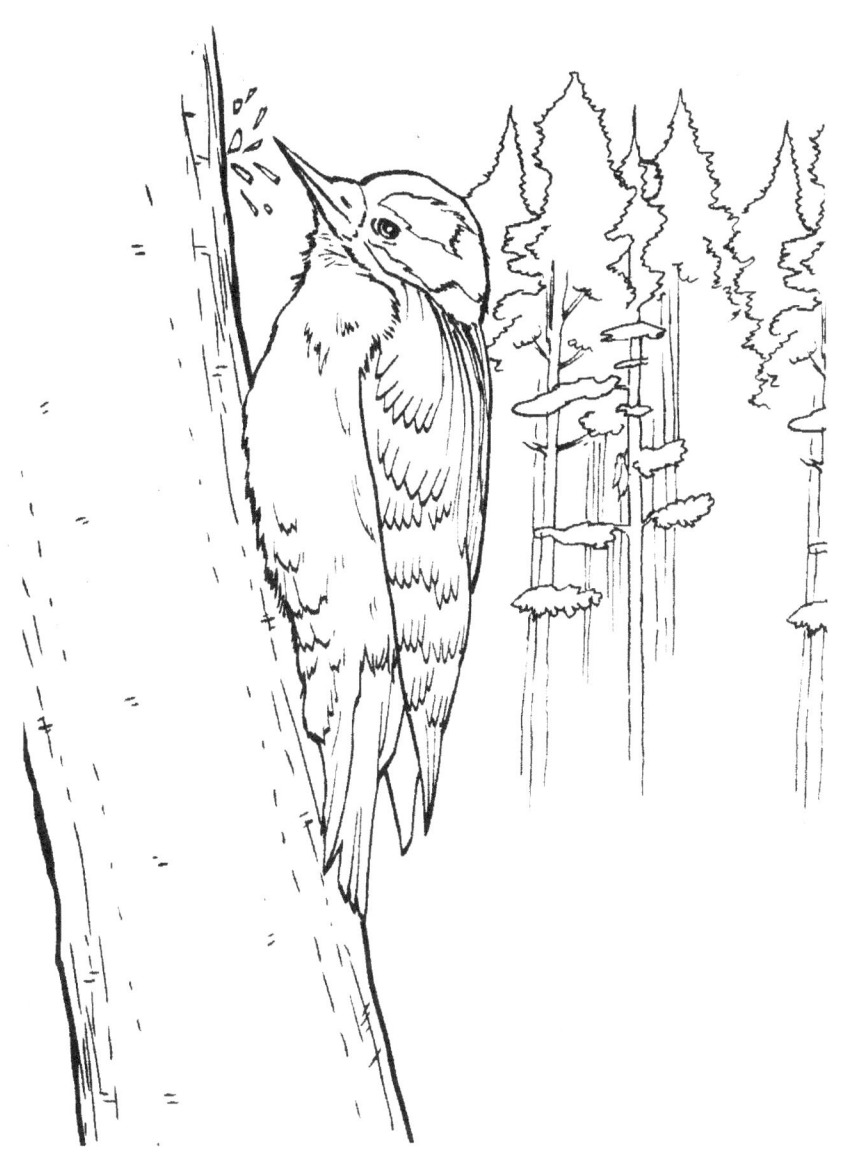

Woodpeckers are not often seen on the ground.

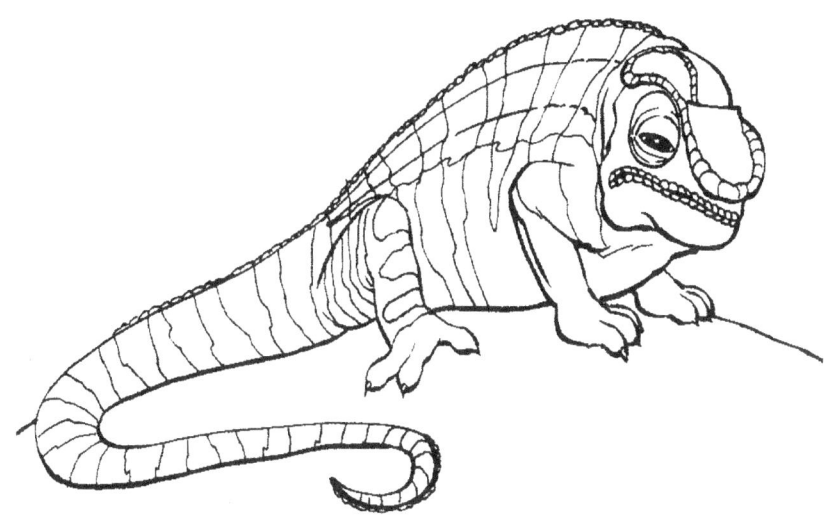

Chameleons change their skin color to adapt to their environment

www.ingramcontent.com/pod-product-compliance
Lightning Source LLC
Chambersburg PA
CBHW071418210526
45465CB00001B/449